Praise for *Half the Battle: Overcoming Life's Hidden Hurts*

I'm so thankful to my friend Jon for writing this book. These words will bring freedom to all of us and will cause us to follow Jesus with new fervor and zeal. Jon is a brilliant communicator, theologian, and pastor. We need this book!

Brady Boyd
Author of *Addicted to Busy, Fear No Evil*, and *Sons and Daughters*
Senior Pastor, New Life Church

Jon Chasteen is my dear friend and spiritual son. He has a gift for uncovering dynamic biblical principles and relating them in a very practical manner that we can all understand and apply to our lives. I highly recommend this book to you. It will bless you!

Jimmy Evans
Best-selling Author and Speaker
Senior Pastor, Gateway Church

I have yet to read a book regarding inner healing that is so practical, applicable, and precise. The use of Scripture, clinical concepts, and real historical events combine to captivate any reader. This book encourages emotional wellness, and the principles included here can be applied to almost any life situation. I will most definitely be adding it to the reading list at my private practice and in the classroom.

Cassie Reid, Ph.D., LPC-Supervisor
Author of *Unwrapped: Open the Gift of Holiday Sanity*
Director of Marriage and Family Therapy, The King's University

Jon's message celebrates a Savior who, having experienced much pain and rejection, compassionately turns to us and says, "Bring Me to your pain." Jon encourages us that Jesus isn't repulsed by our stench; instead, He comes close and invites us into our own resurrection story. *Half the Battle* gives us not only hope for healing but also the practical tools to walk in freedom.

Dino Rizzo
Co-Founder and Executive Director of ARC
Associate Pastor, Church of the Highlands

We all experience battles in life. Instead of acknowledging our pain, though, we often try to stuff it deep down inside and pretend it never happened. But here's the good news: you can be victorious in battle and free from pain! In his new book, *Half the Battle*, my good friend Jon Chasteen explains how you can find hope, healing, and complete freedom in Jesus.

Robert Morris
Best-selling Author of *The Blessed Life, Beyond Blessed,*
and *Take the Day Off*
Founding Lead Senior Pastor, Gateway Church

Dr. Jon Chasteen

Half the Battle

Overcoming Life's Hidden Hurts

Dr. Jon Chasteen

Half the Battle

Overcoming Life's Hidden Hurts

Foreword by Craig Groeschel

with Study Guide

Half the Battle: Overcoming Life's Hidden Hurts

Published jointly with Gateway Press and TKU Press

ISBN: 978-1-951227-27-2 Hardcover
ISBN: 978-1-951227-28-9 eBook
ISBN: 978-1-64689-045-3 Audiobook

We hope you hear from the Holy Spirit and receive God's richest blessings from this book by Gateway Press. We want to provide the highest quality resources that take the messages, music, and media of Gateway Church to the world. For more information on other resources from Gateway Publishing®, go to gatewaypublishing.com.

Gateway Press, an imprint of Gateway Publishing
700 Blessed Way
Southlake, Texas 76092
gatewaypublishing.com

Printed in the United States of America

20 21 22 23 — 5 4 3 2 1

TABLE OF CONTENTS

FOREWORD

My pastor used to say something that always bothered me. Every time he shared this idea, I wanted to argue, push back, and tell him all the reasons why he was wrong. Unfortunately, my older and much wiser pastor was probably right when he said, "Most people are either coming out of a battle, they are in the middle of a battle, or they will soon enter into a battle." Ouch.

I hope you aren't in the middle of a challenging season in your life. But sadly, the odds are that you might be. You could be facing a health challenge. You might be struggling to stay afloat financially. You could have a relationship that you value that has taken a hit. You might be fighting spiritual battles that no one else can see but you cannot ignore. And even if things are running smoothly right now, you could be facing a challenge around the corner.

Here is some good news: you have this book in your hand. Please believe me when I tell you that this is a power-packed, spiritually encouraging, battle-preparing book. This book is crammed with rich Bible teaching. It's full of life-giving and relatable stories. It is a manual for warfare and for healing. This book could be a gift from God just for you, giving you exactly what you need to heal the hidden hurts and stand strong when you'd rather hide.

I love this book for many reasons. First, I love it because I love the author. Jon is unquestionably one of the most humble, godly, and passionate Jesus followers I know. You can't tell from his photo, but he's tall. Really tall. And strong. Really strong. (We work out together when he's in town, and we make loud grunting noises just because it's fun.) But his physical strength and stature aren't nearly as impressive as his spiritual strength and faith in God. Jon is a man of prayer. He's generous. He's bold. And he's sensitive to God's voice.

When Jon told me that he was considering writing this book, I told him to stop considering and start writing. What God has done in Jon's life is something that needs to be shared with as many people as possible. Jon knows the healing power of God first-hand. With God's help, he's overcome trauma, trials, addictions, and strongholds.

This isn't a book for casual reading. It's going to push some of your buttons and take you to places in your soul that you would probably rather avoid. Why? Because this book is full of truth, and truth can be uncomfortable. It takes courage, honesty, and vulnerability to open your heart to God's message of healing.

Here is my challenge to you: keep reading. Push through the discomfort. I promise it will be worth it. Allow the Holy Spirit to speak to you through these pages, and your life will be changed for the better. Will you still face battles? Yes. They are an unavoidable part of life on this earth. But the way you face battles will be different. No longer will fear keep you captive. No more will discouragement hold you back. Instead, you will march toward the enemy with all the authority that belongs to a child of God, and you will declare, "Enough! Your control over me ends now."

It's time to embrace the healing power that Jesus paid for on the cross. May God's protection and peace cover you as you begin this incredible journey to freedom.

Craig Groeschel
Best-selling Author and Leadership Expert
Senior Pastor, Life.Church

ACKNOWLEDGMENTS

I HAVE MUCH to be thankful for when it comes to the making of this book. First and foremost, I thank the One who gave it to me. While this book is by no means the chief authority on any subject, I do believe it is a Spirit-inspired word that God revealed to me. Without God and His Scriptures, this book would not exist.

To my amazing wife, Michele. You never signed up for this crazy ministry ride we have found ourselves on. You have endured so many things and encouraged me constantly. You are an inspiration, and without your love and support I wouldn't be half the man I am.

To my kids, Corey and Jace. I pray this book is a seed even to the two of you. That you will see not only the message of this book but also the work behind it. I pray that everything I do on this earth will plant a seed that will bring fruit in your future ministries.

To my parents, John and Becky Chasteen, who pastored for 22 years and were an amazing influence in my life. Thank you for training me in the ways of the Lord.

Thank you to Victory Church for trusting me to lead. Pastoring this church family has been one of my greatest joys. Pastor Dale Swanson, Pastor Oscar Ortiz, and Pastor Wade Smith: You guys are my best friends and also my warriors in the trenches of ministry. We have been through many battles, trials, and toils that have bonded us in a way that can never be undone. You are incredible leaders and friends.

Thank you to Pastor Craig Groeschel and Pastor Jimmy Evans. Your willingness to be my pastor, friend, and mentor has shaped me and formed me in ways you will never know. You both saw something in me before I saw something in myself.

Thank you to Gateway Church and Pastor Robert Morris. Your investment in me has been life changing. The honor to lead The King's University alongside one of the greatest churches is an absolute dream come true.

Thank you to the leadership and staff at Gateway Publishing for your work in making this book become a reality.

1

BEFORE THE BATTLE

HOW DO YOU feel about the word *battle*? If you're like most people, you're probably not too fond of it. You would much rather think about being blessed, happy, or successful. (And let's be honest—who wouldn't?) But you still opened this book, which leads me to one of two conclusions: you are facing a battle right now, or you want to be prepared for one when it does come. Perhaps it is a strained relationship, a crippling addiction, or a devastating diagnosis. Battles can be brief or drawn-out, minor or major, simple or incredibly complicated. No matter the situation, though, one truth remains constant: without a battle, there can be no victory.

The children of Israel were no strangers to battles. Not only the kind you face with a sword but also the kind you face with a soul. They suffered as slaves in Egypt for centuries, then spent 40 years wandering through a barren wilderness. And their battles were only just beginning. The Israelites were an interesting group; Scripture repeatedly refers to them as a "stiff-necked people." Time and time again they rebelled against God and tried to do things their own way. But because they were His chosen people, the Lord graciously came to their rescue every time they truly repented. If you study the children of Israel throughout the Bible, you will begin to see that they are eerily similar to another group of people—us!

Without a battle, there can be no victory.

God promised the Israelites a land "flowing with milk and honey" (Exodus 3:8). The Israelites referred to this location as the Promised Land. I am sure they pictured it as the place where they could finally find rest. It is probably similar to a teenager who can't wait to get out of his parents' house and get his own place. Only later does he find out that this "promised land" requires work, bills, and responsibility. Imagine the day the Israelites crossed the Jordan River on dry ground. They thought, *Finally! We've crossed over to the other side. We're in the land flowing with milk and honey—the Promised Land.* And what was waiting for them? **A battle**. You know what? I can't take the suspense. Let's fast forward the story and see what happens at Jericho.

> When the trumpets sounded, the army shouted, and at the sound of the trumpet, when the men gave a loud shout, the wall collapsed; so everyone charged straight in, and they took the city (Joshua 6:20).

The trumpet sounded, the people shouted, and the wall collapsed. The Israelites charged in and took the city. They got past what had been holding them back. This is what I am believing for you in whatever you're facing too. If we were to fast forward your story to the end, I believe your walls will fall. I believe your marriage will be healed, your addiction will be loosed, your calling and career will become clear, and you will be healed in Jesus' name. But in order to get to that point, there are some things we can't pass over. I just jumped from Joshua chapter 3 to chapter 6, but some very important events happened in chapters 4 and 5—events that made chapter 6 possible. Maybe your walls haven't fallen yet because you've tried to skip ahead to the end. Could God be waiting for you a few chapters back?

I totally get it, by the way. Chapter 6 gets all the attention. It is the one that's been preached from platforms and placed on Sunday School felt boards for decades. It's the story that is put on paintings, coffee mugs, and posters. However, while Jericho's defeat was a public spectacle of God's awesome power, this victory came only after *half the battle* had already been fought. The first part of the battle did not take place outwardly for all to see. Instead, it was done in secret. Let's rewind the film and go back to see this hidden struggle.

AN UNEXPECTED BLADE FOR BATTLE

The walls of Jericho were breached without the use of a single blade. After seven final laps around and a loud shout, "the walls came a-tumbling down." (Anyone else remember that song from Sunday school?) However, there was a blade involved in the battle *before* Jericho. This blade was not used on the enemy but on the Israelites themselves.

Joshua 3 records the children of Israel crossing the Jordan River at flood stage. This had to be one of the most miraculous and joyous occasions for them. After all, they had been in the wilderness for 40 years! The previous generation had died, and a new generation was walking into the Promised Land they had heard about their entire lives. In chapter 4 the Israelites stack up rocks as a memorial of this commemorative day. Then chapter 5 takes a sudden and direct turn:

> At that time the Lord said to Joshua, "Make flint knives and circumcise the Israelites again." So Joshua made flint knives and circumcised the Israelites at Gibeath Haaraloth (vv. 2–3).

Ouch! I bet they didn't see that coming. Why in the world would God do this now? Remember, of those who came out of Egypt, all the men of military age died in the wilderness. They were circumcised, but all the men born since then were not.

Let's pause a moment to remember how circumcision even started. We have to go all the way back to Genesis 17, when God made a promise to Abraham.

> This is my covenant with you and your descendants after you, the covenant you are to keep: Every male among you shall be circumcised. You are to undergo circumcision, and it will be the sign of the covenant between me and you (vv. 10–11).

Circumcision is the sign of the covenant between God and His people. Before the Israelites went into battle against Jericho, God wanted to remind them of His promise: *You are children of God. You are a chosen people. This is a covenant relationship. You don't go into battle by yourself. I go into battle with you.*

If you are a man reading this book, take a deep breath. I am happy to report that circumcision is *not* a requirement for you to be a follower of Christ (see Acts 15). Can I get an AMEN? But notice what the prophet Jeremiah writes about circumcision:

> For thus says the Lord to the men of Judah and Jerusalem:
> "Break up your fallow ground,
> And do not sow among thorns.
> **Circumcise yourselves to the Lord,**
> **And take away the foreskins of your hearts,**
> You men of Judah and inhabitants of Jerusalem,
> Lest My fury come forth like fire
> And burn so that no one can quench *it*

Because of the evil of your doings" (Jeremiah 4:3–4 NKJV, bold added).

"Take away the foreskins of your heart." Circumcision is not only a literal, physical cutting but also a symbolic, spiritual removal. In Romans 2, the apostle Paul writes:

A person is not a Jew who is one only outwardly, nor is circumcision merely outward and physical. No, a person is a Jew who is one inwardly; and circumcision is circumcision of the heart, by the Spirit, not by the written code (vv. 28–29).

Another translation says, "It's the mark of God on your heart, not of a knife on your skin, that makes a Jew" (MSG). It's a circumcision of the heart.

I don't know why God chose this awkward parallel. He could have used something far easier for pastors to talk about in church or write about in books. However, if you will bear with me, there are some really beautiful analogies to be found on this topic. Think about what circumcision required in the Israelites' day and time. If you were an adult male, you had to invite other people into a very private setting for the circumcision to take place. Picture a grown man walking up to Abraham or Joshua. It took extreme humility to reveal the most private part of yourself to someone else and allow them to cut you. Circumcision of the heart is a similar exercise in humility. Any time God begins to deal with things in your heart, guess what? You have to humble yourself and be willing to bring them to Him. You have to lay down your pride and acknowledge that you've done some things wrong.

The place of circumcision was concealed under articles of clothing, hidden so no one could see it. Circumcision of the heart is no different. In most cases, the things God is looking to cut away from your heart are very private. It's the stuff we cover up. It's the stuff we try to hide and ignore. I'm talking about the issues you know you have but no one else knows you have. I'm also talking about the issues you may not realize you have but everybody else around easily recognizes in you. Pardon my use of the word considering the topic, but circumcision requires you to "expose" yourself enough to allow a cutting away to happen. It requires exposing pain. It requires exposing pride, greed, lust, lies, and anything else you've been using to cover up the secret places of your heart.

Not only was it concealed and very private, but the place of circumcision was a sensitive area. Every man reading this book knows what I'm talking about. I'm sure the Israelite men probably thought, *Wait, you want to take a blade **there**?! No thanks. We're good!* Now think about that in terms of a heart issue. I don't know what your particular pain is, but I know it is sensitive. Maybe it was an abusive situation, in which the one person who was supposed to protect you actually harmed you. Or perhaps you were rejected by someone who promised to be there for you. Do you need to forgive someone but struggle with the idea because they definitely don't deserve it? May I be so bold to suggest that anytime you become easily upset by or overly sensitive to any subject, person, or circumstance, chances are there is something in your heart that needs to be cut away.

We all have issues. We all have things in our hearts that God wants to cut away. My friend Carlos Whittaker wrote an amazing book titled *Kill the Spider.* In it he talks about how God walked him through the process of what I am calling circumcision of the heart. Carlos explains that we often try to clean ourselves up by our own ability. We are fine for a little while, but then we fall right back into temptation. It is like sweeping away cobwebs in the corners of our soul. We clean everything up, but the next morning we find that the spider has woven the same web all over again. Carlos suggests we stop focusing on cleaning up the cobwebs and start concentrating on killing the spider. Only by killing the spider can we prevent the cobwebs from returning. I highly recommend this book.

The things that hold us back are not drinking issues, drug issues, anger issues, or greed issues. No, we have heart issues. Many of the problems we see in people today are merely outward expressions of what is going on inside. But here's the good news: God is after our hearts. I am convinced that God wants your heart more than anything else on the planet. He isn't after your money, time, career, kids, or even marriage. He just wants your heart. Why? Because if He gets your heart, then He gets everything else too. As a parent, my number one prayer is that my kids will give God their whole hearts. It is more important than their grades, friends, behaviors, careers, future spouses, or anything else on earth. If God possesses your whole heart, everything else falls into place with His timing, will, and purpose.

Another interesting perspective on circumcision is *who* performs the procedure. I'm guessing a man who agrees to be circumcised must really trust the person holding the blade. He had better have a steady hand. In Romans 2:29, the apostle Paul writes that circumcision of the heart is performed "by the Spirit." Isn't that comforting? There is a reason God is referred to as the Great Physician. He wants us to know that He can be trusted with the knife.

Jesus said,

> I am the true vine, and my Father is the gardener. He cuts off every branch in me that bears no fruit, while every branch that does bear fruit, he prunes so that it will be even more fruitful (John 15:1–2).

You can either be cut back or cut off. Either way, you get cut. This is a perfect mirroring of the original covenant back in

I am convinced that God wants your heart
more than anything else on the planet.

Genesis 17. God tells Abraham, "Any uncircumcised male, who has not been circumcised in the flesh, will be cut off from his people; he has broken my covenant" (v. 14). God is saying to us, *I am shaping you into what I want you to be. In order to do so, I need to trim some stuff in your life. I want to cut some stuff away from you. And if you just let Me, the pruning is going to produce far more fruit than you could ever produce on your own.*

I know this is heavy stuff, but you know what is even heavier? The Jericho battle that is just around the corner in your life. I want you to win all of your battles. And I am convinced that before we ever win the battles in our future and take territory for our marriages, children, churches, finances, and careers, we must first win the greatest battle we will ever fight—the battle within. Once you do, you can finally breach the walls that have held you back for far too long. I love you enough (and the Holy Spirit does too) to come alongside you and say that there are some things in your heart that God wants to cut away. God wants to cut away unforgiveness. He wants to cut away bitterness. He wants to cut away the things you've used to mask the real issue just under the surface. It's not about the addiction, the anger, the loneliness, or the depression. It's not a matter of you just being you. There are some deeper heart issues that God wants to address.

There's a passage in the New Testament that shows us how greatly Jesus desires our hearts. One of my mentors showed it to me, and it is a really powerful text. Here's the context of the scene: Mary and Joseph have brought the baby Jesus to the Temple in Jerusalem to be presented to the Lord. While there, they meet a godly man named Simeon, who shares this prophetic word:

> This child is destined to cause many in Israel to fall, and many others to rise. He has been sent as a sign from God, but many will oppose him. As a result, **the deepest thoughts**

of many hearts will be revealed. And a sword will pierce your very soul (Luke 2:34–35, bold added).

Jesus came to this earth for your heart. And not just a piece of it. God wants complete access to every dark, dusty, and cobweb-filled corner. He wants us to be willing to expose the awkward and sensitive places in our hearts. His purpose is not to shame us but to purify us.

The English word "heart" in this text comes from the Greek word *kardi*. This is where we get the word "cardio." It refers to the most inward part of a person. The word "reveal" in the text is the Greek word *apocalypto,* which means 'to take off the cover.' Jesus came to take the cover off our hearts, reach our most inward parts, and heal us from the inside out. He wants to heal your past, your pain, and all the things that have led you to this point.

The Holy Spirit comes to us in a loving, kind way, much like I hope I'm delivering this message to you. If you ever feel as if God is beating you over the head with a hammer, that is *not* the Holy Spirit. The Holy Spirit isn't a bully, and He doesn't function that way. No, He is gentle, kind, and incredibly patient. You have a loving heavenly Father who is willing to walk with you every step on this journey. He can be trusted with the blade. Your job is to climb up on the table, expose the tender, broken, and rotten places in your heart, and allow Him to do surgery. This is the most important battle you will ever fight.

TAKE TIME TO HEAL

Joshua 5:8 says, "After the whole nation had been circumcised, they remained where they were in camp until they were healed." Before they could enter into the Promised Land, the Israelites had to wait for the process of healing. The Hebrew word for wait is *qavah*, and it has two definitions. The literal meaning is 'to bind together like a cord by twisting.' Ecclesiastes 4:12 says, "A cord of three strands is not quickly broken." Think about what that means for us. While we're waiting on God to get us to our Promised Land, we're not waiting without purpose. God is twisting and strengthening us like a cord that will not easily break. He does this so that when the time comes to bear the weight of the battles to come, the cord is strong enough to carry the load. In my waiting, I can rest assured that God is strengthening and preparing me. **Without the wait, I won't be able to bear the weight.**

The figurative definition of *qavah* is 'to expect.' While I'm waiting, I can be expecting. David spent much of his life waiting to see God's promises fulfilled, but he didn't wait impatiently. Instead, he waited *expectantly*.

> I remain confident of this:
>   I will see the goodness of the Lord
>   in the land of the living.
> Wait for the Lord;
>   be strong and take heart
>   and wait for the Lord (Psalm 27:13–14).

> In the morning, Lord, you hear my voice;
>   in the morning I lay my requests before you
>   and wait expectantly (Psalm 5:3).

I think it must be something like pregnancy. Now, I'm no medical doctor, and I certainly have no experience being pregnant. But Michele, my amazing wife, gave birth to our two children (Corey and Jace), and I had a front row seat to the entire pregnancy process. With both children, the doctor gave us a due date. Anyone who has ever had a baby knows that a due date is just an *estimated date*; there is no guarantee the

**Without the wait, I won't be able
to bear the weight.**

baby will be born on that particular day. The baby could come days or even weeks early or late. Corey, our first child, was born over two weeks after her due date. But guess what. The extra waiting did not change our expectation. We knew she would come when the time was right.

This is how waiting on God feels at times. We don't know exactly when He's going to show up, but I promise you this: *He's going to show up.* Therefore, wait on God in the same way you'd wait for a baby to come—with great expectations! Michele and I did not wait to buy a crib, clothes, diapers, or that little thing that sucks the snot out of babies' noses until our children were born. While she was still pregnant, we went to several different stores and walked around with that fun little scanner, registering for all our wants and needs. Why? Because even though we did not know the exact time and date of the baby's arrival, we knew the baby was coming, and we wanted to be prepared. So, yes, wait on God to show up in your situation, but wait with great expectation and prepare for His arrival.

Why is learning how to wait well so important? This may come as a surprise, but for the rest of your life, you will be waiting on God to do something. Once He answers the prayer you're waiting on now, guess what is just around the corner? Waiting on Him to do the next thing. We need to learn to do this well.

The Israelites had to learn this too. They finally healed from their circumcision, and what was next? More waiting. They would arrive at Jericho for their first battle, but instead of charging in, God would have them wait. For six days, the only thing the Israelites were allowed to do was march around Jericho's wall once a day. Then on the seventh day, they had to march around it seven times. Do the math. One march times six days, plus seven more marches. That makes 13. They walked around this stupid thing 13 times, and nothing happened. Not one brick moved.

It would have been nice if a layer of bricks fell off the wall with each lap around. At least then the Israelites would have seen progress and had a morale boost. They would have thought to themselves, *This is really hard, but the wall is falling. Just a few more laps to go.* But it didn't happen that way in the battle of Jericho, and it doesn't seem to happen that way in our lives and circumstances either. I'm sure the Israelites just wanted to get the fighting started already. It would have been easier (and less frustrating) to take matters into their own hands. But God said, "Just walk around this thing and wait on Me to move." They had to wait.

Something powerful happens when we're waiting. If you're struggling in the waiting process today, let me encourage you. **While you're waiting, God is working.** I don't know when the walls you are marching around are going to crumble, but I promise you this—they will fall down. In the meantime, be faithful and wait.

THE FIRST WALLS TO FALL

There they sat on the banks of the Jordan River, healing from their circumcision. I believe this was the bloodiest and most difficult battle the Israelites ever faced. The greatest breach was not the walls of Jericho in chapter 6; it was the walls of their hearts in chapter 5. Let me show you this moment of breach. I must have read this verse hundreds of times over the years, but I missed it every time until now.

> Then the Lord said to Joshua, "Today I have rolled away the reproach of Egypt from you." So the place has been called Gilgal to this day (Joshua 5:9).

Did you catch that? **"Today** I have rolled away the reproach of Egypt from you." Why does God say "today"? After all, the Israelites had left Egypt over 40 years earlier. Yes, it was a terrible, cruel place, but the generation that experienced that pain had died in the wilderness. These newly-circumcised Israelites had never even been to Egypt. So why did God choose to bring it up now? He had removed His people from slavery, but a piece of slavery still remained in them. God was telling them, *I removed you from slavery 40 years ago, but today I am going to remove slavery from you. I removed you from the painful situation 40 years ago, but today I am going to remove the painful situation from you.*

Isn't this a perfect picture of us? No matter how long you've been on this earth, you've been through your own wilderness. You have your own list of things that you were a slave to, and you've had your own guilt, shame, and rejection. Although you may not be living in your Egypt anymore, I would suggest that many of us are just like the Israelites. We've carried the reproach of our past with us. God removed you from that abusive situation years ago, but the abuse remains inside. The abortion was 10 years ago, but the pain and sorrow from it hasn't gone away. The divorce was 20 years ago, but it still stings. The devastating circumstance is in your past, yet the destruction and damage linger. It took the Israelites *40 years* to tear down the walls of their hearts. I am convinced that God was more concerned about those walls than the walls of Jericho. **You can never tear down the walls of Jericho unless you first let God tear down the walls of your heart.**

You have to understand what this word "reproach" means. It is the Hebrew word *cherpah*, and it means 'scorn, shame, disgrace.' God says, "Today I have rolled away the scorn, shame, and disgrace of Egypt from you. You have carried this shame generation after generation, and today is the last day you carry

You can never tear down the walls of Jericho unless you first let God tear down the walls of your heart.

it." Most of these Israelites were born in the wilderness, but they still carried the reproach from their fathers and mothers. It had been passed down from generation to generation. Many times, we are haunted by the same challenges and difficulties that our parents faced. And rather than deal with our greatest enemy—the enemy within—we focus on the Jericho in front of us. *God, please fix my marriage. God, please fix my finances. God, please fix this wall that's in front of me that I can't figure out.* But God loves us too much to "fix" it. He knows you will never be able to face the enemy behind the Jericho walls of your life until you have faced the enemy behind the walls you have erected in your heart. There's an enemy inside that you have to fight first.

When we carry Egypt with us, it influences every aspect of our lives. Relationships. Career. Finances. *Everything.* We bring our pain with us, and despite our best efforts to control it, pain always affects our purpose. I remember when I first became a senior pastor. I stepped into leadership in a brutally difficult situation. The founding pastor of the church was (and is) a great man of God, but he made a giant mistake in his marriage. This moral failure cost him his position at the church. While the situation was painful for everyone involved, one particular pastor on staff was especially devastated. He had moved his family across the country to be at the church and had been promised many things.

One day after an all-staff meeting, this pastor came into my office and started ripping into me. I could have snapped back and put him in his place, but I sensed something else going on. *Pain.* After all, this wasn't his normal character. Instead of responding to his tantrum, I simply said, "I am sorry." I told him I was sorry that he was promised things that could never have been fulfilled. I was sorry that he had to move his family across the country. I was sorry that his life, expectations, and plans were being messed up because of someone else's mistake. And you know what he did? He broke down and cried. Why?

Because I spoke to the sensitive area of his heart. God wanted to circumcise his heart in this area and heal it. Today this man is completely whole, healed, and doing incredible ministry at another church.

Pain will cause people to react in a multitude of ways. As a leader, when you see poor performance, angry outbursts, or other toxic behaviors, do not respond to the outside without being mindful of the inside. If we will begin to see people's issues as pain and not as personal attacks on us, then we can begin to offer real ministry. Perhaps the reason God has brought a difficult person to serve under your leadership is to help them face the battle within so they can later conquer many future Jerichos for the kingdom.

2

THE STENCH BEHIND THE STONE

LET'S RECAP WHERE we are. The Israelites have crossed the Jordan River and resealed their covenant relationship with God through circumcision. In Joshua 5:9, the Lord says to them, "Today I have rolled away the reproach of Egypt from you." The words "rolled away" are not random. The verse goes on to say, "The place has been called Gilgal to this day." The Hebrew name *Gilgal* literally means 'circle of stones' or 'rolled away.' This is a very intentional use of words. As I began to meditate on that, I began to think about other times in Scripture where similar words were used to describe a situation. When was there a circular stone that needed to be rolled away? My mind went immediately to the cross. After Jesus was crucified, His followers put His body in a tomb; on Sunday morning, however, the stone was "rolled away."

Then my mind went to another biblical story about a stone being rolled away from a grave. It is the story of Lazarus (see John 11), and I believe it speaks to us about the things we carry today. Here is some brief context of the situation: Lazarus falls ill, and his sisters, Mary and Martha, send for Jesus. They know Jesus is a healer because they have seen Him heal the sick many times. Surely Jesus will be willing to rush over and perform a house call on His close friend Lazarus. Much to their surprise, though, Jesus delays and only arrives after Lazarus had been dead for four days! Oh, the sisters are *not* happy. Martha comes out to meet Jesus and declares, "If you had been here, my brother would not have died" (John 11:21). Mary later falls at Jesus' feet and echoes her sister's words. That brings us to this passage:

> Therefore, when Jesus saw her weeping, and the Jews who came with her weeping, He groaned in the spirit and was troubled. And He said, "Where have you laid him?" They said to Him, "Lord, come and see." Jesus wept. Then the Jews said, "See how He loved him!" And some of them said, "Could not this Man, who opened the eyes of the blind, also have kept this man from dying?" Then Jesus, again groaning in Himself, came to the tomb. It was a cave, and a stone lay against it. Jesus said, "Take away the stone." Martha, the sister of him who was dead, said to Him, "Lord, by this time there is a stench, for he has been *dead* four days." Jesus said to her, "Did I not say to you that if you would believe you would see the glory of God?" Then they took away the stone *from the place* where the dead man was lying (John 11:33–41 NKJV).

Think about what graves represent. They aren't meant to be opened. Instead, they are sealed, because there's something inside we don't want to experience. It's not pretty. In fact, there is a stench. Mary and Martha were thinking this very thing. Martha's instant reply was: "Lord, by this time there is a stench, for he has been *dead* four days."

STENCH

Stench. What a bizarre yet interesting word. The dictionary defines it as 'a strong and very unpleasant smell.' The kind of thing you want to avoid. Mary and Martha knew all about the stench related to their recently deceased brother, Lazarus. The smell of a decomposing body has to be one of the worst odors on the face of this earth. (Have you ever come across roadkill? Gross!) However, I would like to suggest that perhaps the stench of Lazarus' decomposing body was not the only thing they were trying to avoid. It was not just the stench of a corpse that they put in a dark place and rolled a stone in front of it. Perhaps the stench that got to the sisters the most was the pain in their souls. The pain of having Jesus deny their request. The pain of unmet expectations. The pain of feeling abandoned and forgotten. **For Mary and Martha, the stench of pain was too much to bear, so they put it in a dark place and rolled a stone in front of it.**

What do we do with things that carry a stench in our lives? The things that stink too badly and hurt too deeply? We do the same thing Martha and Mary did. We shove them in a dark place in our heart and roll a stone in front of it. This inner grave becomes an isolated place. A stinky place. *It becomes the stench behind the stone.*

What I have found in my years of pastoring is that there are very few people who do not carry some sort of stench. Something that happened in their past refuses to go away, and because they do not know what else to do with it, they shove it in a deep, dark place in their heart. For some it is a sense of abandonment or rejection. Perhaps you were given up for adoption, or even though your parents were there, they didn't provide for your physical, emotional, or spiritual needs. Maybe you worked faithfully for your company for years and years, only to end up getting let go. For others it is an abusive situation. Perhaps it was sexual, emotional, physical, relational, or spiritual abuse. Regardless of the details, at some point the pain becomes too much to deal with, and the stench becomes too great. So we stick our pain in a dark place and roll a stone in front of it. The results of this differ from person to person, but the effects of such pain are always visible. Some people respond by becoming angry at the world. They are incredibly pessimistic and negative about everything. Others respond by becoming distant and guarded or even arrogant and narcissistic. It has always been interesting to me how people respond to pain differently.

I have a friend who is from Mexico. Let's call him Nick, even though that is not his real name. He has been living here in the United States for over 20 years trying to obtain his citizenship. He pays his taxes, has a driver's license, owns a house, and is a law-abiding resident. Yet he remains in a continual legal loop, unable to receive citizenship. Nick has always been a man of great character and integrity, but I began to notice a pain in his soul. It was as if God had given me a window into Nick's heart, and I could now see his stench behind the stone. I had always thought of my friend as a humble and gracious person because he was willing to do anything for anyone at any time. But God showed me that this outward display of "humility" was actually covering up a deep sense of shame and rejection.

One day I was sitting in a room with Nick, and I sensed the Holy Spirit nudge me to say something. So I looked at my friend and said, "You have no reason to be ashamed. You have done nothing wrong, you're a good man, and you belong in this country." Nick did not say a single word; he simply began to weep. Later, he told me that his challenges to get his citizenship and the way people treated him because of his struggles with English as a second language had caused significant pain in his life. Shame and rejection had created an internal message

We all carry something from
our past that hurts.

that there was something wrong with him. Without realizing it, Nick had come into agreement with the devil that he did not belong, had no place, and was less than enough.

Like my friend, we all carry something from our past that hurts. We stick it in a dark place, roll a stone in front of it, and declare to anyone who passes by, "This place is inaccessible. This place is impenetrable. This is a place that you don't belong, so don't you dare try to access it." I think you know what I am talking about. There is a person in your life who has a certain topic that you know better than to bring up. If you dare mention that name or situation, all hell breaks loose. Why? Because the loss was too great, and the pain was too deep. In order to cope, they have erected a wall around their heart.

You may be thinking, "I have to get this book for so and so! They have to read this!" And that's great. Of course, I want people to hear this message. However, my greater preference is that *you* would take a good look at yourself too. *We all stink.* We all have a little stench here and there. Circumcision of the heart is a **continual** process, not a one-and-done event. For the rest of our lives, we will be climbing up on God's surgical table, trusting the Great Physician with the blade, and asking Him to cut away things in our heart that do not belong there.

JESUS IS NOT OKAY WITH PERMANENTLY SEALED TOMBS

In the story of Lazarus, we quickly learn that the Lord is not okay with permanently sealed tombs. Jesus comes to confront the stone and deal with the pain they tried to hide. I think the Resurrection is further proof of that. After Jesus died on the cross, His body was shoved in a dark place, and a stone was rolled in front of the entrance. That didn't last long, though.

John 1:5 in the Passion Translation reads, "And this Living Expression is the Light that bursts through gloom—the Light that darkness could not diminish!" Jesus came to conquer the grave and destroy darkness. **He was not okay with His permanently sealed tomb, and He is not okay with yours either.**

However, there is one person who is a big fan of your sealed tomb. His name is Satan. Satan would be much more satisfied if that stone remained sealed over your heart, and he will do everything he can to keep it that way. He makes the stench so bad and the pain so sensitive that your heart becomes like an infected wound. Have you ever experienced an infected wound? My friend's son recently got a staph infection in his leg. It didn't look very bad from the outside—only a small red sore. Just under the skin, however, a very dangerous infection was spreading quickly. If ignored, it would have caused severe and life-altering problems. In order to stop the infection and save the leg, the wound had to be opened. The young man had to brave the pain and trust the doctor and his scalpel.

TAKE HIM TO THE PLACE OF PAIN

The story of Lazarus is a physical picture of a spiritual truth. Jesus wanted to visit the dark place in front of which Mary and Martha had rolled a stone, and He wants to visit your place of pain too. He wants to come and expose those areas of your life that you've locked and sealed away—not to remind you of the trauma but to alleviate the pain forever. He wants to do away with it and resurrect something in you that has been dead for far too long. He wants to bring life back to your spirit, soul, and body. Watch how Jesus approached Mary and Marth's pain:

When Jesus saw her weeping, and the Jews who had come along with her also weeping, he was deeply moved in spirit and troubled. "Where have you laid him?" he asked (John 11:33–34).

I think it's interesting that Jesus asked where they had put Lazarus. As if He didn't already know. Jesus could have walked right by Mary and Martha, marched up to the tomb, and said, "I'll fix this whole situation." But He didn't. He stopped and asked their permission to go there. Can I tell you something? Jesus knows where you've hidden your pain. Maybe you hid it so long ago that you've forgotten the exact place, but Jesus knows. And with more compassion and love than you could ever imagine, He is asking your permission to go there. Jesus says, "Show Me where your faith ended. Take Me to the place where you lost all hope and quit believing. Let Me see where the pain was so real that you didn't know what else to do with it but shove it in a dark place and roll a stone over it to cover up the stench."

I love Mary and Martha's response because ours must be the same: "Come and see, Lord" (v. 34). *We've already given up all hope, Jesus, but we'll still show You. We really don't think there's any hope in this situation, but we're going to show it to You anyway.* Perhaps the only thing more captivating than their willingness to take the Lord to their place of pain was Jesus' response to it. John 11:35, the shortest verse in the Bible, says, "Jesus wept." Mary and Martha humbled themselves and agreed to take Him to the place where their faith had ended. Where they had given up hope. Where they had lost all dependency on Jesus and who He was. This would have been a perfect opportunity for Him to rub their noses in their doubt. To criticize them, rebuke them, or even sit down and teach them. This would have been a great spot for a sequel to the Sermon on the Mount. But Jesus didn't do any of those things. Instead, Mary and Martha's pain became His pain.

Jesus knows where you've hidden your pain.

You have to remember that while Jesus is fully God, He also became fully human. Our Savior is not just some guy on a throne in Heaven looking down on us like little ants. When He came to earth, Jesus faced every temptation we face and felt every emotion we feel. So how does He respond to your pain? The same way He did to Mary and Martha's pain. On their walk to the tomb, He wept with them. He weeps with you too. When you decide to show Jesus your stench behind the stone, the journey there will not be met with shame, criticism, or rebuke. It will be a journey filled with compassion, love, and grace.

EVEN NOW

In verse 21, Martha tells Jesus, "Lord, if you had been here, my brother would not have died." This is such a raw and authentic cry. It reveals her pain, and it also shows us the way in which we can talk to our Creator. I'm sure you can relate to this frustration when you think about your painful past. Why didn't God show up? Why didn't He keep that situation from happening? But right in the middle of her doubt, Martha finds the ability to rise above it and declares, "But I know that even now God will give you whatever you ask" (John 11:22).

"Even now." What a ridiculously powerful phrase. It is a pivotal moment for Martha. *This is the place where her doubt and her faith intersect.* I don't know what your situation is. But I do know that if you will escort Jesus to your place of pain, He is an "even now" kind of God. Even now, 20 years after the divorce. Even now, 10 years after losing a loved one to cancer. Even now, 50 years after your mother abandoned you. Even now, 30 years after your uncle sexually molested you. *Even now, God, I'll take You to this place of pain that I've locked away inside my heart. I'll reveal it to You. Even now, God, I believe there's something that can happen here.*

JESUS ADDRESSES THE STENCH

In verse 35 we see Jesus weeping with Mary and Martha on their way to the tomb. However, once they arrive at the tomb, a transformation occurs.

> Jesus, again groaning in himself, came to the tomb (John 11:38 NKJV).

At first glance, we would assume that His "groaning" is a continuation of the weeping, but this word actually has a different meaning. It comes from the Greek word *embrimaomai,* which means 'to be very angry, to be moved with indignation.' One definition even uses the words "to snort in" as a horse would do when extremely agitated. *Wait a minute,* you object. *Jesus was angry? I thought Jesus was perfect. He never got mad.* The verse does not say Jesus lost His temper. It says He was angry. You know why I think Jesus was angry? This is simply my opinion, but I think He was angry because He caught a whiff of the stench behind the stone. The One who represented life was standing in a place that represented death. The Light of the world was standing in a place of darkness. The enemy had tried his best to come in and bring death, and that pained Jesus so badly that it gave Him righteous anger.

A PURPOSE FOUND IN PAIN

Verse 38 ends with these words: "It was a cave with a stone laid across the entrance." These simple words give us a glimpse of the scene. Here was the place of darkness and loneliness. The stone across the entrance signified that all hope was lost. This had to be the place where the pain was the greatest.

You may have a loved one who has gone on to be with the Lord. Sometimes you go to their grave to pay your resects, have a conversation, pray, or simply be silent. Regardless of the why, your visitation to that place floods you with emotions. For Mary and Martha, the scene at the tomb had to elevate their pain level to a roar. If this book is even remotely taking you to your place of pain, it is not an easy process. Our pain can really shout at our souls. C. S. Lewis said, "We can ignore even pleasure. But pain insists upon being attended to. God whispers to us in our pleasures, speaks in our conscience, but shouts in our pains: it is his megaphone to rouse a deaf world."[1]

Sometimes it is in your place of greatest pain that you will hear the voice of God the loudest. I know that was the case for the prophet Elijah. In 1 Kings 18, Elijah faces off with the prophets of Baal on Mount Carmel. God sends fire down from heaven to consume Elijah's sacrifice, thus proving that "the Lord is God" (v. 40). Elijah then kills the prophets of Baal. In 1 Kings 19, Queen Jezebel declares she is going to murder Elijah, so the prophet flees for his life. Verse 4 says, "He came to a broom bush, sat down under it and prayed that he might die." The pain drives him so far that he becomes suicidal.

God then directs Elijah to a cave on a mountain. Having just witnessed the awesome power of the Lord on Mount Carmel, the prophet probably expected a mighty demonstration. A "great and powerful wind" comes by (v. 11), followed by an earthquake and a fire. But God isn't in any of them. Instead, He comes in a "gentle whisper" (v. 12) and gives Elijah much-needed strength, encouragement, and wisdom.

Pain was the megaphone that drove Elijah to encounter God. Perhaps your pain will do the same for you. Perhaps your place of pain is where you will encounter God in a way you would never have imagined. A visit to your stench behind the stone could be the only thing that stands between you and your next

Sometimes it is in your place
of greatest pain that you will hear
the voice of God the loudest.

victory in battle. Are you willing to roll away the stone and let Jesus into the hidden places of your life?

Surrender. That is all God ever asked any of us to do, isn't it? We have to come to the understanding that without the Light of the world invading our lives, we are weak and hopelessly in the dark. Jeremiah 17:9–10 reveals our dilemma:

> The heart is hopelessly dark and deceitful,
> a puzzle that no one can figure out.
> But I, God, search the heart
> and examine the mind.
> I get to the heart of the human.
> I get to the root of things,
> I treat them as they really are,
> not as they pretend to be (MSG).

We think we can hide our pain by acting like we've got it all together. I love that God says, "I treat them as they really are, not as they pretend to be." When we roll a stone in front of our pain, we pretend to be someone or something that we're not. Let's be honest—it's easy to put ourselves together and present a perfect (or at least functional) life. It's easy to present a good marriage on social media. It's easy to portray financial success through your purchases. It's easy to fake happiness through a text or phone call. But God cuts right through the façade. We may be able to fool everyone else, but the Great Physician does a spiritual MRI of our hearts and sees our problems for what they really are. He gets right to the heart of the pain that every one of us carries.

Jesus is ready to heal you. The question is, are you willing to climb up on the surgery table and allow Him to circumcise your heart? God's hand is both steady and ready, but there is a part we must play in this process.

THE PART WE PLAY

Let's move on in the story of Lazarus. Jesus looks at the tomb and says, "Roll the stone aside" (John 11:39 NLT). This seems strange to me. I mean, He doesn't really need their help to get the stone out of the way, does He? If I were Jesus, I would have just pointed my finger at the stone and made it explode into a million pieces, displaying all my glory. In fact, I might have made the entire world move in slow motion so everyone could watch in wonder as the stone disintegrated into dust. But Jesus doesn't do that. He asks these weak, insignificant, and helpless people to move it. Remember, they are still mourning their loss, and He is asking them to exert themselves. Why would He ask them to do such a thing? Hopefully by now you know Jesus well enough to know that He doesn't waste a thing. Everything He does is by design and for a purpose.

Now let's talk about that stone. Stones that sealed tombs were *very* heavy. No one wanted a stone that would just roll away at the slightest breeze. The thought was, "Once we roll this stone in place, no one is ever going to enter this tomb again." It would definitely take some work for Mary and Martha to roll the stone aside. But Jesus wanted them to participate in this exercise. He wanted them to be a part of it.

Hopefully you're catching on to the symbolism here. Your stone is heavy too, isn't it? It seems impossible to move. Have you ever thought, *God, You can move it for me, can't You? Why can't I just say a simple prayer and be over it? Why can't I just read a book or take a class and be good to go?* But for some reason, Jesus is always involving us in His work within us. In essence, what Jesus was telling Mary and Martha was this: *I need you to do what you can do. Then I will step in and do what you can't do. I know moving the stone is going to be really difficult. You may have to grunt, strain, sweat, and be uncomfortable. But if you will do what you can do, I will step in and do what you could never do in a million years. Because you can move a stone, but you can't resurrect a dead body.*

You cannot heal the pain you feel inside—only Jesus can do that. But can you take Him to your place of pain? Can you roll the stone away? Can you tear down the walls you have built around your heart? I know what you're thinking. *Yes, I might be able to do that, BUT you don't understand just how painful my situation is. My stone is heavier than you could imagine.*

My kids have experienced their fair share of bumps, bruises, and skinned knees. Whenever they get injured, they run to me, holding whatever hurts. But the moment I try to assess the damage, they pull back and exclaim, "Don't touch it!" They come to the right place, but they don't want to go through the pain of dealing with the hurt. And before you say, "I'm tougher than that!" let me remind you that we do the exact same thing as believers. Life knocks us down, so we cry out in protest and slap the most readily accessible bandage on it. But when our heavenly Father asks us to remove the bandage so He can heal us, we shrink back and hide. We think, *God, You don't understand the pain I feel. You don't understand what I'm going through.* Here's the truth, though: God does understand. Better than anyone else (even better than you). And if you will take off that bandage, which actually isn't hiding anything, and reveal your pain, He will heal you.

No one else had to know that the Israelites who crossed the Jordan River were uncircumcised. It's probably not a subject that the surrounding nations would have ever brought up. But God knew, and in His infinite love and wisdom, He wasn't willing to let it go. Before they could fight a single soldier or win a single skirmish, the Israelites had to humble and expose themselves. It was incredibly awkward and difficult but also absolutely necessary. Circumcision of the heart is a similar endeavor. It would be extremely humbling to put this book down and call a trusted friend or family member to expose your pain. (I'm not saying you have to do that right now. I believe God will let you know when to share and with whom to share.) Here's what I know to be true: **healing and pride aren't compatible.** We have to pick one or the other. If we want to be healed, we have to take our pride, set it to the side, and tell it to shut up. Then we have to crawl up on the surgery table, roll back the stone, and say, "God, this is the place of my pain."

PROTEST

I love how human Mary and Martha were. They were personal, face-to-face friends with Jesus—the Savior of the world—yet they still dealt with the same doubts and fears that we experience today. Jesus asks them to roll away the stone in front of their brother's tomb, and you would think their immediate response would be "Yes, Lord." But that's not what happens.

> But Martha, the dead man's sister, protested, "Lord, he has been dead for four days. The smell will be terrible" (John 11:39 NLT).

Jesus asks them to do something, and Martha protests. She doesn't outrightly refuse, but she lets Jesus and everyone else around the tomb know that she is not in agreement with this plan. Has someone ever come so close to a painful area in your life that you tossed up an emotional red flag and said, "Whoa, man! Let's not go there"? Why would you react that way? Because you have the same fear that Martha did. *The smell will be terrible.*

Jesus didn't need to be taught the scientific process of decay that occurs in a deceased human body. Lazarus certainly wasn't the first dead person He had ever encountered. To lecture Jesus, who was there when the foundation of the world was laid, seems preposterous. I can't put too much blame on Martha, though. As ridiculous as her response is, it's a very *human* response. It's human to pull away from pain. Why do you think people often avoid going to the doctor, even though they know something is physically wrong? Because they're afraid that the cure will hurt worse than the pain. I wouldn't be surprised if people pulled away from this book (if they haven't already stopped reading it). I know I'm digging into deeply personal issues that people spend their entire lives avoiding. We're humans, so we protest. But there is one thing that is for certain: if we ever want to be healed, we have to deal with the pain.

If we ever want to be healed,
we have to deal with the pain.

3

DEALING WITH REJECTION

I WANT TO take this chapter to talk about something that I believe is one of the primary weapons of the enemy—*rejection*. It's a term we use often in our language, but rarely do we stop to think about the significant effects of it. At first glance, it does not seem like that big of an enemy. You would think that the devil's greatest weapons would be some of the harder stuff, such as porn, drugs, or even pride. However, let's take a closer look at the characteristics of our enemy. Time and time again, the Bible describes the devil as a deceiver. In fact, in his very first interaction with humans, the devil lied to Eve in the Garden of Eden. The apostle Paul warns believers that the devil "masquerades as an angel of light" (2 Corinthians 11:14). He is a deceitful little devil, isn't he?

According to the Oxford Dictionary, the definition of deceitful is 'guilty of or involving deceit; deceiving or misleading others.' The devil deceives us into thinking everything in our lives is normal and fine, but he's actually doing significant damage behind the scenes. If I were the devil, that is what I would do. I would attack you with things you never saw coming. I would come at you in a way to infect you without you even knowing you were infected. I would do everything in my power to ensure that you did not know you needed help.

SEEDS OF REJECTION

The seed of rejection is far smaller than the fruit it produces. Like a virus or bacteria, a microscopic thing can enter a host and create sickness or even death. There have been many plagues throughout history, but one of the deadliest was the Bubonic Plague (also known as the Black Death). In case you aren't familiar with this topic, here is a brief overview from History.com:

> The Black Death was a devastating global epidemic of bubonic plague that struck Europe and Asia in the mid-1300s. The plague arrived in Europe in October 1347, when 12 ships from the Black Sea docked at the Sicilian port of Messina. People gathered on the docks were met with a horrifying surprise: Most sailors aboard the ships were dead, and those still alive were gravely ill and covered in black boils that oozed blood and pus. Sicilian authorities hastily ordered the fleet of "death ships" out of the harbor, but it was too late. Over the next five years, the Black Death would kill more than 20 million people in Europe—almost one-third of the continent's population.[2]

For centuries, it was thought that rats (or the fleas on rats, more specifically) were responsible for the spread of this disease. Then, in 1888, French bacteriologist Alexandre Yersin discovered the bacillus (a rod-shaped bacterium) *Yersina pestis*.[3] This bascillus travels pneumonically (through the air) as well as through animals.[4] That means that a person didn't necessarily have to be bit in order to be infected with the plague; all they had to do was breathe contaminated air. Quite recently (in 2017), a study published in *Proceedings of the National Academy of Sciences* ruled out rats as the primary carriers of

The seed of rejection is far smaller than the fruit it produces.

the disease. Instead, researchers concluded that it was the fleas and ticks on humans that led to the plague's rapid spread.[5]

For those who got the Bubonic Plague, a simple bite from a flea or a breath of polluted air was all it took to become infected. Rejection works in a very similar way. Many times, it begins as the simple bite of a spouse's momentary failure to meet our physical or emotional needs. Or the inhalation of toxic, hateful words spewed by a loved one in a heated moment. The poison-filled sting of abusive actions or words can take root in our hearts and begin to cultivate an infection. Over time this infection begins to stink. It becomes a stench in our mindset and attitude.

People thought rats were the main cause of the outbreak of the Black Death, but it turned out to be humans who spread it. We can try to ignore our pain, pass it off as normal, or blame other things in life for making us the way we are. However, that doesn't change the fact that we humans are often the primary carriers of the disease of rejection.

Once a person was exposed to the plague, as many as seven days would pass with no apparent side effects.[6] Then the host would experience a sudden onset of fever, chills, headache, fatigue, malaise, and muscle aches. And that was just the beginning. The Bubonic Plague is named for the buboes (swollen lymph nodes) that develop in a person within a week of being infected. Located in the groin, armpit, or neck, buboes are similar in size to a chicken egg and are both tender and painful to the touch.[7]

Before the panic surrounding the epidemic ensued, a person infected with the plague likely had no idea how sick he or she would become. Many of the early symptoms could have been mistaken for the common cold or the flu. Once again, rejection has many similarities. Maybe you felt the unexpected "bite" of a friend's words or actions and thought, "Ouch! That was weird." Or perhaps you have experienced so many "bites" in your life that the latest one didn't even seem that traumatic. Either way, we try to blow it off and tell ourselves, *No big deal. I can get through this. I will just move on and forget it ever happened.* We put the rejection in a dark place, roll a stone in front of the entrance, and walk away.

Notice where the most painful symptoms of the plague developed: groin, armpit, and neck. These are places of privacy and sensitivity; they're concealed and off limits. You might think, *The neck is not a private area.* Oh really? Next time you're on an airplane, reach over the seat to that stranger of the opposite sex sitting in front of you. Grab their neck and see how they react. Or you can save yourself a lot of trouble and just take my word for it. As humans, we don't like others coming near our sensitive places, and in regard to rejection, your heart is the most sensitive place you have. That is why the enemy works so hard to infect it. He knows we won't want to show anyone and get the help we really need.

Rejection is the reason why circumcision in the Old Testament was so important. God established circumcision to remind His people of their covenant relationship with Him. Let's read His promise to Abraham one more time.

> This is my covenant with you and your descendants after you, the covenant you are to keep: Every male among you shall be circumcised. You are to undergo circumcision, and it will be the sign of the covenant between me and you (Genesis 17:10–11).

God was telling Abraham, "This is between you and Me. This is not about performance, ritual, religion, or works. This is about relationship." The Abrahamic covenant even serves as a foreshadowing of the relationship between Christ and His bride (the Church). God wanted His people to have a continual reminder of their relationship with Him. Why would they need it? Because the Israelites would face rejection over and over again. Before they crossed the Jordan River and before they traveled through the wilderness, they were slaves.

> Now Joseph and all his brothers and all that generation died, but the Israelites were exceedingly fruitful; they multiplied greatly, increased in numbers and became so numerous that the land was filled with them. Then a new king, to whom Joseph meant nothing, came to power in Egypt. "Look," he said to his people, "the Israelites have become far too numerous for us. Come, we must deal shrewdly with them or they will become even more numerous and, if war breaks out, will join our enemies, fight against us and leave the country." So they put slave masters over them to oppress them with forced labor, and they built Pithom and Rameses as store cities for Pharaoh (Exodus 1:6–11).

Did you see it? Complete and utter rejection. The whip was a daily reminder that the children of Israel were not accepted in Egypt. The message was loud and clear—*You are less than. You are worthless. You have no value.*

For the Israelites suffering in Egypt, the covenant of circumcision was more than a ritual or tradition. It was a symbol of hope and acceptance. Circumcision reminded them who they were, to whom they belonged, and most importantly, with whom they were in relationship. It was a message from God that said, "I know this world has rejected you, but you are My children, and I accept you." This message is for us too. If you are a believer in the Lord Jesus Christ, you are a child of God. We are a "chosen people, a royal priesthood, a holy nation, God's special possession" (1 Peter 2:9). And you don't have to be Jewish either. Romans 11 and Ephesians 2 tell us that Gentiles

I know this world has rejected you,
but you are My children, and I accept you.

(non-Jews) have been grafted in to receive the promises of Israel.

We may never experience actual, physical slavery like the Israelites did, but we still have lives that are full of rejection. That is why it is so important that we *continually* allow God to circumcise our hearts. We need the constant reminder that we are accepted by the One who matters most.

THE FRUIT OF REJECTION

In agriculture, fruit is simply a by-product of a seed that was planted and a root system that was established. Jesus told His disciples, "A good tree produces good fruit, and a bad tree produces bad fruit. A good tree can't produce bad fruit, and a bad tree can't produce good fruit" (Matthew 7:17–18). When we experience someone who is producing bad fruit, whether it be a negative attitude or behavior, we should shift our attention to the root and find the seed that produced that root. It would be easy to look only at the outside and label the person with anger issues, money issues, or whatever other issues seem to apply. But if we want to get the truth of the matter, we have to get our hands dirty and dig below the surface.

When the root cause of someone's negative fruit is exposed, you will probably uncover issues such as bitterness and unforgiveness. However, if you will take the time to go a little bit deeper and pull back just one more layer, you will often find that what started the whole thing was a tiny, inconspicuous seed. This is the seed that the enemy—that deceitful little devil—loves to plant. It is the seed of rejection.

PAIN IN THE BRAIN

Like many things in life, science usually comes along with "revolutionary and groundbreaking" discoveries that simply confirm what God's Word has been revealing to us for centuries. Renowned psychologist, author, and speaker Dr. Guy Winch has studied the subject of rejection extensively, and he says, "Rejections are the most common emotional wound we sustain in daily life."[8] Scientists are discovering that the effects of rejection on the brain are much more significant than they previously realized. Dr. Mark Leary, Professor of Psychology and Neuroscience at Duke University, explains, "It's like the whole field [of psychology] missed this centrally important part of human life."[9]

According to Dr. Winch, "fMRI studies show that the same areas of the brain become activated when we experience rejection as when we experience physical pain. This is why rejection hurts so much (neurologically speaking)."[10] Rejection and physical pain share the same pathways to the brain, which explains why "as far as the brain is concerned, a broken heart may not be so different from a broken arm."[11]

What is the fruit of rejection? How does it manifest in our lives? Scientists have now proven that rejection is directly linked to anger and aggression. A 2001 report issued by the United States Surgeon General concluded that "rejection was a greater risk for adolescent violence than drugs, poverty, or gang membership."[12] Rejection isn't something we simply grow out of either. All too often we encounter stories of spurned spouses or laid-off employees who lash out in extreme and violent ways. Dr. Winch says, "Even mild rejections lead people to take out their aggression on innocent bystanders."[13]

While the scientific study of rejection is fascinating, let's return our focus to the spiritual components of this issue. Rejection enters our lives and produces tragic and devastating fruit. You can see why the enemy would make this one of his greatest weapons in warfare against us. So if bitterness and unforgiveness are the root and rejection is the seed, then what is the soil? After all, without the right soil, a seed won't grow. Matthew 13 talks about the importance of where a seed falls. If it is going to sprout and grow, then it must fall on fertile soil.

I am no expert in this field, scientifically speaking. After all, my doctorate is in university administration. However, I believe God has given me a fresh revelation on this topic, and my years of pastoring have allowed me to see this at work in many ways. Is it possible that the soil in which rejection grows best is fear? If not the soil, then perhaps fear is the fertilizer that makes it grow. Let me give you a few examples. Perhaps deep down, someone believes they are not lovable and fears they will not be accepted. Any rejection received from a parent, friend, or spouse serves only to feed this fear, and the seed of rejection begins to grow. What if someone believes they are not smart or talented enough and fears someone will notice their inadequacy? Then getting laid off becomes much more than just losing a job. It is a rejection that confirms a deep fear, grows into a root of bitterness and unforgiveness, and produces the fruit of distrust in bosses, companies, and working society in general. Many times (I would even say most of the time), the fruit of pain can be traced back to a root, a seed, and perhaps even the soil in which the seed was planted.

I believe social media makes people today more vulnerable to rejection than ever before in history. Dr. Winch writes, "Our risk of rejection used to be limited by the size of our immediate social circle or dating pools. Today, thanks

**Is it possible that the soil in which
rejection grows best is fear?**

to electronic communications, social media platforms and dating apps, each of us is connected to thousands of people, any of whom might ignore our posts, chats, texts, or dating profiles, and leave us feeling rejected as a result."[14] We subject ourselves to thoughts of rejection by people who have no idea they are even rejecting us. This confirms our subconscious fears that we are alone and no one likes us. The devil is always working angles to try to get us to come into agreement with these lies. He is constantly planting seeds of rejection in the soil of our fears.

So what happens when someone who should have accepted you rejects you? What happens when someone who should have been a father to you fails you? What happens when someone who should have made you feel secure violates you? I would have to write an entirely different book to list all the different fruits that can come from the seed of rejection. But if someone came to me and said, "Jon, what is the single most debilitating fruit that manifests from a seed of rejection?" I would immediately answer, "Insecurity." I believe we all struggle with insecurity on various levels. However, those who suffer from significant rejection tend to have elevated signs of it.

Insecurity is an extremely bizarre topic. One of the strangest things about it is that insecurity can create strengths. Yes, I said *strengths*. At least at first glance they look like strengths. I know a young man who is one of the most gifted businessmen I have ever seen. Everything he touches turns to gold. He can organize projects, manage and lead teams, and perform in ways that most only dream of. There is no task he cannot accomplish, no project he can't conquer, and no goal he can't meet. And this "gift" has made him significant amounts of money. But at a closer glance, although his projects are successful, the collateral damage that happens with everyone this man comes into contact with is catastrophic. As a result, he struggles with drug abuse and debilitating self-hatred on a level that is hard to describe. After getting to know him better, I learned he grew up with a father who constantly nagged at him. His father would say things such as, "You will never succeed. You will never be anything in life." Wow! Imagine the pain of hearing those words. Sadly, many of you can. This man experienced deep father wounds with the knife of rejection and grew up with the fear of never being good enough. His fertile soil of fear was the perfect place for the seed of rejection to grow, and a bitter root began to develop. Rejection fostered an intense longing to be accepted and a deep desire to prove his father wrong. Yes, this man is now materially successful, but it has come at great personal cost.

Insecurity often grows from the same seed of rejection that is planted in the soil of fear. However, it can produce a plethora of different types of bad fruit. Let me say it again—I am no expert in the field of psychology. These are simply my thoughts based on my years as a pastor. In my experience, I have found that insecurity typically manifests itself through two types of people. The first type is the one I will call the *overcompensator.* Many times this person can seem extremely confident and maybe even arrogant or narcissistic. Rarely will they ask, "How are you doing?" and actually be interested in hearing your answer. You know that any interaction or conversation with this person will be centered on *their* family, *their* career, and *their* achievements. And it's not as though they are trying to be mean about it. There's just a constant (albeit subconscious) need to overcompensate in the area of self-promotion.

The other type of insecure person I often see is the *self-deprecator.* This person is the extreme opposite of an overcompensator. It is not that they are just quiet or socially reserved, although many times they are both. My wife is an introvert, but while she would prefer to stay out of the spotlight, she is still a secure and confident person. Self-deprecators, on the other hand, constantly have to be talked out of the gutter. They are incapable of seeing their own gifts and talents and have little self-worth on a day to day basis.

Think about this: the very first murder in the Bible happens just four chapters into Genesis. Creation is barely finished, and humans are already killing each other. You remember what happens, don't you? Cain and Abel, the sons of Adam and Eve, bring their offerings to God. God accepts Abel's offering of the firstborn of his flock but rejects Cain's offering of crops. This rejection makes Cain so angry that he ends up killing his brother. Now, please hear me. I am not saying that if you don't let God heal the stench behind the stone, then you're going to become an axe murderer. I am simply helping you see the connection between the seed of rejection and the poisonous fruit it produces.

THE REJECTION CORRECTION

Here's the good news: even when our rejection causes us pain and produces bad fruit, we serve a God who redeems and restores. Enter the story of Jacob and Esau. If you attend church, then you've probably heard plenty of sermons on these two brothers. Most of the time, Jacob is presented as the hero, and Esau is the guy we never want to be like. And in the context of most sermons, that is the moral of the story. Esau was the firstborn son of Isaac and Rebekah. In those days, the position of a firstborn son came with a full and undeniable claim to the family inheritance. However, in a moment of weakness, Esau made a massive mistake and sold his birthright for a bowl of soup. Then in Genesis 27, Jacob tricked their father into giving him Esau's blessing by making Isaac

Even when our rejection causes us pain
and produces bad fruit, we serve a God who
redeems and restores.

think Jacob was Esau. When Esau later arrived at his father's bedside to receive the blessing belonging to the firstborn, Isaac realized Jacob's deception. Look at the words of Isaac to his son Esau and imagine the rejection Esau was inflicted with in that moment.

> Isaac said to Esau, "I have made Jacob your master and have declared that all his brothers will be his servants. I have guaranteed him an abundance of grain and wine—what is left for me to give you, my son?" (Genesis 27:37 NLT).

The very thing that rightfully belonged to Esau was taken from him. The father who was there to protect and provide had seemingly denied and abandoned him.

> Esau pleaded, "But do you have only one blessing? Oh my father, bless me, too!" Then Esau broke down and wept (Genesis 27:38 NLT).

This was the moment of pain. The moment of affliction. The moment where a seed of rejection was planted deep in Esau's heart. Unfortunately, this seed grew into a stench of its own. You can see the rotten fruit that rejection produced just a few verses later.

> From that time on, Esau hated Jacob because their father had given Jacob the blessing. And Esau began to scheme: "I will soon be mourning my father's death. Then I will kill my brother, Jacob" (Genesis 27:41 NLT).

The fruit came bursting forth as anger. Even beyond anger, it was hatred. Perhaps you know someone who carries this type of anger or hate towards someone or something. Maybe you can relate to Esau in the frustration of your situation. And while

Esau did make mistakes, he was the one who was wronged. He was cheated and abandoned.

However, there is another part of this story that you rarely hear told. If you look at the Scriptures closely enough, you will see a beautiful picture of redemption—the same kind of redemption that awaits us. After Esau wept in verse 38, Isaac gave a final remark that held the key to his firstborn's potential deliverance.

> Finally, his father, Isaac, said to him, "You will live away from the richness of the earth, and away from the dew of the heaven above. You will live by your sword, and you will serve your brother. **But when you decide to break free, you will shake his yoke from your neck**" (Genesis 27:39–40 NLT, bold added).

Did you see it? Woven into the bad news of this situation was a clue. A silver lining of sorts. A giant, enormous BUT. Isaac was telling his son Esau that when he decided to break free from the yoke of bondage, he could. It was a choice. I believe this message is just as much for us today as it was for Esau back then. We carry heavy burdens on our shoulders, but we were never meant to carry that weight. The weight becomes a stench, and this stench becomes our Achilles Heel.

I believe Esau did eventually shake the yoke of bondage off his neck. I believe he did go on to have a blessed and abundant life. Why do I think that? Because many years later, Esau and Jacob reunited. After deceiving his father and brother, Jacob ran away to live with his uncle Laban. Jacob worked for Laban for 20 years. During that time, he married both of Laban's daughters (Leah and Rachel) and accumulated large amounts of livestock, sheep, goats, and servants. Things became tense between Jacob and Laban, though, so Jacob decided to take his family and all his possessions and return to his homeland (see Genesis 31). There was just one problem—Jacob would have to face Esau. The one he cheated. The one from whom he took everything. The one who was so angry that he planned to kill Jacob.

Jacob's only hope was to appease his brother Esau with gifts.

> Then he selected these gifts from his possessions to present to his brother, Esau: 200 female goats, 20 male goats, 200 ewes, 20 rams, 30 female camels with their young, 40 cows, 10 bulls, 20 female donkeys, and 10 male donkeys (Genesis 32:13–15 NLT).

This was not a small offering. There is no way to know the exact value in today's economy, but I did find a few people who attempted to do the math. Most of them calculated the value of the herd at approximately one million dollars in today's economy. Regardless of the exact amount, we know this was no small gift Jacob was offering.

Scripture doesn't tell us about Esau's journey while Jacob was away. We are left thinking he was still angry, bitter, and ready to kill his brother. But watch Esau's response to Jacob's gifts:

> "And what were all the flocks and herds I met as I came?" Esau asked. Jacob replied, "They are a gift, my lord, to ensure your friendship." "**My brother, I have plenty**," Esau answered. "Keep what you have for yourself" (Genesis 33:8–9 NLT, bold added).

He had enough that he wasn't even tempted by this enormous peace offering from his brother. I believe Esau had redeemed what had been stolen. I believe he picked up on the clue his father gave him. Esau realized he had a stench behind the stone that needed healing. I believe he climbed up on the Great Physician's table and allowed God's steady hand to perform a spiritual heart surgery. And because he was willing to humble himself and forgive his brother, Esau experienced abundant blessing and favor. Not necessarily from the hand of his earthly father but from the hand of his heavenly Father. I think Esau came to the realization that even though he had experienced pain, rejection, and loss, he gained something far greater than anyone on earth could offer him. He received comfort, acceptance, and blessing from his heavenly Father.

Maybe the key to overcoming the fruit of rejection in our lives is simply coming to terms with not who we are but Whose we are. When we decide to shake off the yoke of bondage that weighs us down, we allow the unending, undeniable, and unrelenting love of Christ to set us free from the spirit of rejection.

THE KEY

I used to drive this tiny, old, and rusty 1994 Honda Accord. Old and the rusty didn't bother me, but since I am 6'7", the tiny part was not very comfortable. Still, this car was the only thing we could afford at the time. One day I was leaving the mall after a failed attempt at shopping for clothes (another big problem when you're 6'7"). I approached my little car, put my key in the lock, and turned it to unlock the door. (Yes, young people, we used to use an actual key to open the car door). I stuck my key in the ignition and started the car. Then I thought to myself, *Wait a minute. What is that smell? What is that trash on the floorboard? Why is there an air freshener hanging from the rear-view mirror? I didn't leave that there.* And then it hit me. *Oh, my goodness, this isn't my car.* It wasn't my car! How did my key open the door and even start the car?! I quickly took the key out the ignition and jumped out of this mystery vehicle. Then I spotted my car three parking spots away. Both cars were the same make and model; they had same paint color and even the same interior (minus the trash of course). I literally got in the wrong car! *I had the right key but the wrong vehicle.*

I wonder if this describes us as Christ-followers sometimes. We know that Jesus is the key to everything we need. He has given us the ability to overcome anything we need to overcome. Scriptures confirms this to us:

> By His divine power, God has given us everything we need for living a godly life. We have received all of this by coming to know him, the one who called us to himself by means of his marvelous glory and excellence (2 Peter 1:3 NLT).

So if we know that we have the right key, then why are we still stuck? Why aren't we going anywhere? We've heard all the Scriptures. We've heard all the Christian sayings and quotes. In fact, we know how to speak the language ourselves. We've sat through every sermon on every topic and can almost preach them ourselves before the preacher even gives the sermon title. Here's what I think: *we spend a large part of our lives trying to use the right key to open the wrong door.* We put the key of Christ in our marriage, but before you know it, we're distracted by our finances, so we put Him over there instead. Then sickness comes, and we put the key of Christ in that area. Now don't get me wrong; Christ belongs in each of these areas. But what if the only thing you need to use the key of Christ for is to open the most important, most locked down door in your life—your heart?

As I mentioned in chapter one, I don't think God is after your marriage or your money. He isn't after your career, your kids, or

God wants one thing and one thing only:
your heart.

even your plans. God wants one thing and one thing only: *your heart*. Why? Because when He gets your heart, He gets your marriage, money, career, kids, and plans too. Your whole heart is all He's after. Only then will it begin to unlock all the other things in your life. But as long as there is a stench behind the stone, you are keeping Him from invading that space. Perhaps this is what Jesus was talking about in Luke 10, when He and His disciples were invited to eat at Mary and Martha's home (before Lazarus became sick). Scripture paints a scene of two different people doing two very different things. Martha was busy at work in the kitchen, cooking and preparing a meal for everyone to eat. Mary, on the other hand, was simply sitting at Jesus' feet. This frustrated Martha, so she complained, "Lord, don't you care that my sister has left me to do the work by myself? Tell her to help me!" (v. 40). Jesus' answer probably surprised her.

"Martha, Martha," the Lord answered, "you are worried and upset about many things, but few things are needed—or indeed only one. Mary has chosen what is better, and it will not be taken away from her" (Luke 10:41–42).

Only one thing was needed. Mary had figured out that the only necessity was giving Jesus her whole heart. The question we must ask ourselves is this: *what part of our hearts are we still holding back from God?*

In Matthew 22, the Pharisees decided to test Jesus by asking Him, "Which is the greatest commandment in the Law?" (v. 36). Jesus answered, "Love the Lord your God with all your heart and with all your soul and with all your mind. This is the first and greatest commandment" (vv. 37–38). All of your heart, all of your soul, and all of your mind belong to Christ, but is there an area in which you've delayed handing over control? Have you given God your *whole* heart? Or are there pieces you still choose to manage on your own? My prayer is that this book begins to reveal the pieces of your heart that are still awaiting circumcision. The areas you have placed in darkness and hidden behind a stone. Make the decision today to give God your whole heart.

4

THE FINAL RESTING PLACE OF PAIN

WHEN I FIRST began teaching on this topic, I was completely overwhelmed by the response. I remember the first time I preached my "Stench Behind the Stone" sermon. It was October 21, 2018, and I was really nervous about bringing this message to the church. As you can see by now, it is a heavy subject. It gets into people's business really quickly. And as we have discussed up to this point, this topic addresses some very sensitive, private, and difficult issues in people's lives. As I preached, people sat there in total silence. I was thinking, *I might have missed it on this one*. They were deathly quiet. However, I have learned over the years that congregations are often quietest when you are preaching what they need to hear. After all, when people are in surgery, they do not talk either.

At the end of the sermon, I gave an opportunity for people to respond by coming forward to the altar area. Our church is accustomed to these altar calls, but we don't have them every week. After I gave the invitation, I was completely overwhelmed by the number of people who came forward. There was no room left in the altar area. People had to fan out far to the right and left. Many were left standing in the aisles because of the gridlock. Hundreds of people responded. Even at the extension campus, there was an overwhelming response to an invitation given over video.

I knew it was a message God had placed on my heart to share. However, now that I had encouraged people to roll the stone back and expose the stench, I had no idea what to tell them to do with the pain. I had walked them through this journey up to this point. I had talked about the Israelites on the banks of the Jordan River. I had gone over the connection of circumcision and our covenant relationship with God, and how these relate to the circumcision of our hearts. I had told them all about the words of God to the Israelites—"Today I have rolled away the reproach of Egypt from you." I had walked them through the story of Lazarus and the stench behind the stone. I had addressed rejection and revealed the schemes of the enemy to plant those seeds that grow toxic fruit in our lives. And people had gotten it. They were on to the devil's lies and ready to do something about it. There was just one problem: I hadn't thought far enough in advance to know where to take them from there.

Throughout the entire week following that sermon, I was inundated with emails, conversations, and questions. The feedback was overwhelming. I felt like I had walked into the enemy's camp, pulled back the curtain, and revealed all his weapons. He wasn't very happy about it either. Something supernatural was taking place. Almost every person who contacted me said something similar to this: "Jon, something happened to me. I have found a pain deep within me that I didn't even know it was there. I remember the rejection. I remember the abandonment. I remember the abuse. And it hurts to bring it back to the surface." And then almost every one of them would say something like this: "I don't know what to do with it. I've tried to forgive them, but the pain remains. I don't know what to do with it."

I've never preached a sermon that prompted more feedback than this one. One lady from Illinois contacted me and said she had simply searched "sermon about inner healing" on the internet. She said my "Stench Behind the Stone" sermon popped up, and her marriage was completely restored and healed as a result of it. God had revealed some things to both her and her husband, so they rolled the stone away and began dealing with their pain. Another lady wrote this: "I remember the exact words of rejection that my mother told me when I was eight years old, and it scared me. I have never forgiven her. What do I do with this pain?" I had a licensed counselor tell me that she has all of her patients who struggle with inner healing watch that sermon before she begins counselling them.

Story after story after story began to emerge. I was completely overwhelmed and, quite honestly, a little concerned. At this point I was thinking, *Okay guys, I'm just a pastor. I'm not a psychologist, and I'm not sure how to help you from here.* But I knew I was going to have to address these questions from the pulpit and bring clarity and insight on a deeper level to help these people move past their pain. I had no idea what to preach, but as always, the Holy Spirit provided. Over the next few days, through Scriptures and conversations with spiritual mentors in my life, God began to give a fresh revelation to me that provided answers for the questions and confusion. The following week, I got up on the platform and preached a message titled "The Final Resting Place of Pain." The following is that message.

LET'S GET REAL

I truly believe we all have hurts that we carry with us. Some are small wounds of rejection that happen on a daily basis; others are cataclysmic events that shape us in ways we haven't even realized. Many times, we've carried our pain so long that we've forgotten it is even there. I'm going to challenge you with something before you read any further. Seriously, put this book down for a moment and do something for me.

Take out a piece of paper or open the notes app on your phone, tablet, or computer. Ready? I want you to write down your pain. No one but you is ever going to see this, so you can be brutally honest here. Who or what has hurt you? What rejection have you experienced? It doesn't matter if it was small or huge. You might have been removed from the situation, but a piece of the situation still remains in you. Write down the rejection. Write down the hurt. You might keep it simple and just write one word. *Father. Spouse. Sibling. Friend. Boss. Stranger.* Or perhaps you will want to go a step further and include some details. I will leave that up to you. But it is important to take your pain out of your subconscious and bring it into the light. Let it become real in front of you, instead of a thought or feeling behind you. I want you to write it down because we are going to take your pain to its final resting place today.

YOU'RE IN GOOD COMPANY

First and foremost, I want you to realize that you are not alone. Many times, hiding our pain in a dark place within ourselves creates a sense of isolation. We begin to believe that we are the only ones who struggle with our pain. We feel all alone in this process, and, therefore, we cannot talk to anyone about it. Elijah felt this way when he was running from Jezebel. The prophet cried out to God, "I am the only one left!" (1 Kings 18:22; 19:10). He felt totally alone and isolated in his pain. Instead of scolding Elijah for a lack of faith, God responded with this encouragement: "I reserve seven thousand in Israel—all whose knees have not bowed down to Baal and whose mouths have not kissed him" (1 Kings 19:18).

God wanted Elijah to know the same thing He wants you to know—you are not alone!

Search through Scripture, and you will find the issue of rejection over and over again. It seems as though anyone who was ever used by God went through a process of feeling rejected. Moses was rejected numerous times throughout his life. When he was a baby, his own mother placed him in a basket and sent him down a river to be picked up and adopted by the Egyptians. Yes, her motives were pure and her actions saved Moses' life, but to a child, it was still abandonment. Moses grew up knowing he was a misfit among the Egyptians. He realized he was of Hebrew decent, and he even killed an Egyptian to keep him from beating a Hebrew slave. However, when Moses tried to stop two Hebrews from fighting, one of the men retorted, "Who made you ruler and judge over us? Are you thinking of killing me as you killed the Egyptian?" (Exodus 2:14). The Egyptians didn't accept Moses, and neither did the Hebrews. Pharaoh heard about the murder, and Moses was forced to flee into the wilderness, rejected and alone.

Remember Hagar in Genesis 16? She was mistreated by Sarah, the wife of Abraham, so she ran into the wilderness. There, God encouraged Hagar and reminded her that He is "the God who sees me" (v. 13).

Remember our discussion earlier about Cain and Abel in Genesis 4? Abel's first fruits offering was accepted by God, but Cain's offering was rejected. Cain's anger led him to murder his brother.

Remember the story of Noah in Genesis 6? He was the nut job who decided to build a boat when it had never even rained. No one believed him, and he spent decades building the ark while experiencing rejection.

How about Joseph in Genesis 37? Talk about rejection! When was the last time your own siblings threw you in a pit, staged your death, and then sold you into slavery?

And don't forget about our friend Esau. He made the bad choice to trade his birth right for some soup, and then his blessing was stolen by his younger brother (see Genesis 25:29–34; 27). Isaac didn't know he was blessing the wrong son, but this still created a deep wound of rejection in Esau.

Need a New Testament example? The apostle Paul was rejected time and time again as he shared the gospel. In 2 Corinthians 11, he writes about being beaten, stoned, and shipwrecked. Paul admits, "I have faced danger from my own people, the Jews, as well as from the Gentiles" (v. 26).

And how could we forget about the disciples? The disciples were rejected everywhere they went. In the book of Acts, they went from town to town to preach the gospel and received rejection from both the people and the governing rulers.

Some of the people I just listed managed rejection well; others did not. My point is this: rejection is not a new thing. You are not alone in this. It is also important for me to tell you that admitting a pain or hurt does not mean you did something wrong. It means someone (or something) has wronged you.

THE BEST COMPANY

Although it might encourage us a little to know that all of these characters in the Bible experienced rejection and pain, perhaps the greatest encouragement is to know that Jesus did too. Yes, Jesus Himself was rejected. The main difference between us and Jesus is that He was blameless. He was fully God, yet He humbled Himself so much that He stepped off His throne in heaven and came down to earth as a human.

The Word became flesh and blood and moved into the neighborhood (John 1:14 MSG).

Admitting a pain or hurt does not mean
you did something wrong. It means someone
(or something) has wronged you.

Jesus was tempted in all the same ways we are tempted. He suffered more than we could ever imagine. Please believe me when I say He understands our pain. Luke 2:5–7 describes the circumstances of Jesus' birth, and they were anything but glamorous. Verse 52 says, "Jesus grew in wisdom and in stature and in favor with God and all the people." He *grew,* just like a regular human. He got taller and smarter. Luke 4 records Jesus' temptation in the wilderness. He didn't eat anything for 40 days, and he "became very hungry" (v. 2). Why was Jesus hungry? Because He had become fully human and was experiencing the weakness of humanity.

I had just a few days left before I had to come back up to the pulpit and preach a sermon to answer the question everyone seemed to be asking—"What do I do with this pain behind the stone I have rolled away?" My wife came to me with this passage of Scripture she was reading and shared how it was speaking to her. It never ceases to amaze me how the Holy Spirit will put on Michele's heart the very topic or thought that I am about to preach on. (Side note: my wife is way smarter and deeper into the thoughts of God than anyone I know. Most of my sermons come from revelations she receives through Scripture. We are a perfect team. She helps me come up with the content and theology, and I'm just the loudmouth that delivers it). Anyway, Michele read me this Scripture from Psalm 118:

> The stone the builders rejected
>   has become the cornerstone;
> the Lord has done this,
>   and it is marvelous in our eyes.
> The Lord has done it this very day;
>   let us rejoice today and be glad (vv. 22–24).

Oh my goodness. That was it! Instantly I knew this was the truth in Scripture I needed. Did you catch it? Jesus was the stone that the builders rejected. Think about all of the times Jesus was rejected.

- His earthly father, Joseph, wanted to break off the engagement to his mother (Mary) when he found out she was pregnant.
- His mother, Mary, had to lay Him in a manger because there was no room in the inn.
- Herod was so jealous at the thought of another king that he ordered the murder of every boy around Jesus' age in Bethlehem.
- The Greeks rejected Him.
- The Romans rejected Him.
- The Jews rejected Him.
- His disciples rejected Him.
  - Judas betrayed Jesus to the Jewish religious leaders.
  - The disciples ran away when Jesus was arrested.
  - Peter denied knowing Jesus, not once but three times.
- The crowds rejected Him.
- The Pharisees rejected Him.
- The Sadducees rejected Him.
- The soldiers at the cross mocked Him by offering Him sour wine (Luke 23:36).
- He was rejected by all of us while He hung on the cross, bearing the weight of our sin.
- Perhaps the worst rejection He ever felt was in the last moments before He died. His own Father rejected him because of our sin that He bore. Jesus cried out, "My God, my God, why have you forsaken me?" (Matthew 27:46).

Many (if not all) of you have felt the pain of rejection. You have suffered through what this life has to offer. Now that you have acknowledged the pain, you're probably asking the same questions as my congregation. *What do I do with it? How do*

I make the stench go away? The moment my wife showed me those verses in Psalm 118, I knew exactly where I could find the answer. It shouldn't have surprised me, either, because it's the same place we find the answer to all of life's difficulties. We just have to look at the only person who ever walked the face of this earth and was blameless in every way. His name is Jesus.

If Jesus experienced rejection on this earth as you and I have but still remained perfect, then we need to ask ourselves this important question: *how did Jesus deal with rejection?* Knowing this will help us to know what to do with our rejection.

Think about this truth. Up to the very last moments of His life on this earth, Jesus was offered bitterness, yet He always refused to accept it. No matter how many times He was rejected, He consistently refused to become bitter. Jesus refused to allow the pain of rejection to hold Him back, even as He was on the cross. Look at the symbolism found in this text:

> The soldiers gave Jesus wine mixed with bitter gall, but when he had tasted it, he refused to drink it (Matthew 27:34 NLT).

Jesus was offered bitterness, but after tasting it, He refused to drink it. Have you ever tasted bitterness? If anyone has ever harmed, abandoned, wronged, or in any other way hurt you, then the answer is yes. There are many things we can do with this bitter drink.

THE HEAVY STONE OF REJECTION

Imagine a large stone—something very heavy, hard, and seemingly immoveable. Now that you have this picture in your mind, mentally write the word *rejection* across the stone. Think back to what you wrote on that piece of paper or in your notes app a little bit ago. That is your stone. It's heavy, isn't it?

Jesus refused to allow the pain of rejection
to hold Him back, even as
He was on the cross.

Let's take a moment and talk through some of the different options of what we can do with our pain and rejection.

OPTION 1: HIDE IT AWAY

The first option we have with this heavy stone is to hide it away. It's far too heavy to carry around with us in our everyday lives, and we don't really want to deal with it anymore. So we find a dark corner in our hearts where we can put it down and cover it up. It doesn't hurt as much when it's over there, so we just keep it hidden.

We don't tell anybody about it. We don't tell anybody about being physically abused. We don't tell anybody about being betrayed by our spouse. We don't tell anybody about the harmful things that our mother or father did to us. We just stow it away. We put it in a dark place and roll a stone in front of it to hide the stench. It's dead, it's decayed, and it stinks. And we would rather do just about anything than deal with it.

Ephesians 5:13 says, "But all things become visible when they are exposed by the light [of God's precepts], for it is light that makes everything visible" (AMP). The problem with the strategy of hiding it away is that the heaviness of the stone doesn't really go away. In fact, it only gets heavier. And the space that it takes up in our hearts doesn't get smaller. It actually grows and begins to impede other things. It becomes heavier and heavier and bigger and bigger until it has no choice but to impact your thought life, your marriage, your family, and your habits. Before you know it, your habits become addictions, and the pain becomes even more unbearable. Needless to say, I do not suggest this option.

OPTION 2: PASS IT OFF

If you do not choose to hide your pain away, then a second option is pass it off. It's too difficult to hide it away anymore, so I am just going to pass my pain off to those around me. I'll pass it off to my spouse, my friends, and my coworkers. This produces an "It's everyone else's fault" mentality. It's my friend's fault that I'm an addict. It's my spouse's fault that I cheat. It's my kids' fault that I lose my temper. It's my parents' fault that I was born on the wrong side of the tracks and can't be successful.

I pass the pain off to somebody else because I can't carry it anymore. The stone is too heavy, and it feels a lot easier to pass the buck to those around me. Many of you have had pain passed to you, and it becomes your pain. Next thing you know, you're passing the pain on to your kids. This is a generational, cyclical process. My pain is passed on to you, but now that I've caused you pain, you turn around and pass the pain back to me—and on goes the cycle.

The problem with this strategy is that the stone still does not become any lighter. In fact, it becomes viral in nature. Think of someone who has the flu. Spreading it to someone else doesn't lessen the effects of the virus on the original sick person. They are still sick, and now so is the newly infected person. The same is true for trying to pass off your pain. It doesn't lessen the weight. You still carry it with you, and now so do the people you love.

Let me show you an example in Scripture. In Genesis 15, God promises Abram that he's going to be the father of many nations. But the promise takes longer than Abram and his wife, Sarai, expect, and it becomes a burden to them. We see some of this frustration begin to come out when they try to pass the burden off to somebody else.

> Now Sarai, Abram's wife, had borne him no children. But she had an Egyptian slave named Hagar; so she said to Abram, "The Lord has kept me from having children. Go,

sleep with my slave; perhaps I can build a family through her" (Genesis 16:1–2).

The pain of rejection will lead you to do things that can never be reversed. Pain leads you to swipe the credit card. Pain leads you to pick up the bottle. Pain leads you to insert the needle. Pain leads you to abuse other people through your words or actions. These are all things that cannot be reversed. Sarai tells her husband to sleep with her slave girl. That can't be undone. Then when Hagar becomes pregnant and begins to "despise her mistress" (Genesis 16:4), Sarai tells Abram that it's all his fault. What is Sarai doing? She's taking the pain of rejection and making her husband carry it. *This is your fault!*

I don't recommend this second option any more than the first. Instead of reducing your pain, passing it off simply multiples it and hurts both you and those around you.

OPTION 3: CARRY IT ALONG

Maybe you can't hide your pain because it's too obvious. Perhaps you've tried passing it off, but the results were disastrous for everyone involved. There is a third option: you can just carry it along. You tell yourself, "This is my problem. I will just carry it and handle it myself." The problem with this option, though, is that it takes you down a long, downward spiral of bitterness.

Bitterness creeps in when we hold on to hurt. You know what I'm talking about, right? You think you have moved on. You might even tell yourself you have forgiven the person who hurt you. But when you see them at the grocery store, you turn the cart in the other direction so fast that someone might think the plague just walked in front of you. Or you see this person post something on Facebook, and you wish you could put a different finger on the *like* button. You wish there was a "You're an idiot, and I wish you would just go away" button.

The pain of rejection will lead you to do
things that can never be reversed.

Know what that's called? A grudge. You can forgive somebody 99.999%, but if you hold on to that last 0.001%, the residue of that stench remains. Sometimes we hold on to a grudge for "just in case" purposes. We think, *I'll keep that in my pocket just in case I need to pull it out to defend myself. That way, I never have to feel the pain.*

Hebrews 12:15 says, "See to it that no one falls short of the grace of God and that no bitter root grows up to cause trouble and defile many." Do you know what will happen if you're not careful? Your grudge will grow up, and it'll get bigger and stronger. And before you know it, it will start manifesting itself. Then you will have to do something to cope with it, because it's become too heavy to carry.

Proverbs 14:10 says it this way:

> Each heart knows its own bitterness,
> and no one else can fully share its joy (NLT).

Pain is a tricky thing because it is invisible. You don't know someone else's pain, and no one else knows your pain. The only way to know pain is to carry it every day. Maybe you know the meaning of that more than you care to admit.

When we choose to carry our pain, we simultaneously commit to repositioning it on a regular basis. Have you every carried something really heavy? If I gave you a small box filled with 10 bricks and told you to carry it across the room, you could probably pull that off without a problem. But if I asked you to carry it across five football fields, that would be different. You could probably still do it. After all, you are pretty tough and strong. But you would have to reposition it from time to time. You might carry it under your left arm, then shift it to your right arm, then put it up on your shoulder and maybe down in front of your waist with two hands. You could get there, but it would take some repositioning of the weight.

Your pain is no different. You can carry it for a while. After all, you are pretty tough and strong. You've been through a lot. But you're going to have to reposition your pain. You might get another self-help book that really does help for a little while. It gives you a place to put the pain for a season. You will be fine for a few days, weeks, or months. After a while, though, even that will get burdensome, and you will have to reposition again. We tell ourselves:

- If I can just make a little more money, then I will be okay.
- It's my career. I just need to find a new job or a new boss.
- I just need a little drink, needle, or pill to help me relax.
- It's my spouse. They just bring me down.

You know what those statements represent? Repositioning your pain. You can carry it how you want. Reposition it all you want. It will still eventually wear you down because you were never meant to carry it in the first place. It's too heavy for you.

Like the first and second options, carrying your pain is a choice you can make. But I wouldn't recommend it. Perhaps there is an alternative option.

REJECTING REJECTION

Before giving you this alternative option, I need to lay some groundwork. I think it's interesting that Psalm 118:22 says Jesus was "the stone the builders rejected." Now back in those days, cornerstones were something very important. Builders didn't lay concrete stem walls and foundations like we do today. It was all about the cornerstone. The builders would go to a rock quarry and walk through the rocks to find one good enough to use as a cornerstone. "No, that one is not good enough. I reject that one." The builder would reject any number of rocks before finding one suitable to build on. Jesus became the stone that the builders—the Pharisees, Sadducees, and rulers of that day— walked up to and said, "No, He can't be the Messiah. There's no way. He's not the one."

But guess what? Those "builders" were wrong. As it turns out, the Pharisees and Sadducees were operating outside their pay grade. They were not qualified to decide who the Messiah was or wasn't. And guess what? *When someone rejects you, you have the ability to reject their rejection.* Who died and made that person the rejection expert? The pain they inflict upon you does not have to have authority over you. The shame you sense does not need to be the shame you allow to take root in your heart. Be careful who you allow to reject you. **Just because somebody rejects you does not mean you have to receive the rejection.** When you keep the rejection, you've hired the wrong builder. You're allowing your life to be marked by the people who walked by you and said, "No, you're not good enough." Watch how Paul describes us in his letter to the Ephesians. He uses the analogy of construction but gives us a glimpse of a different builder who does not reject us in any way:

> You are no longer foreigners and strangers, but fellow citizens with God's people and also members of his household, built on the foundation of the apostles and prophets, with Christ Jesus himself as the chief corner-stone. In him the whole building is joined together and rises to become a holy temple in the Lord. And in him you too are being built together to become a dwelling in which God lives by his Spirit (Ephesians 2:19–22).

Foreigners and strangers are those who have been abandoned, rejected, and left alone. They find themselves in a place they do not belong. Paul is saying this label no longer applies to you. You are not rejected or abandoned; you are a part of the greatest family on earth. We are fellow citizens with God's people and also members of His household. You are part of God's family. You are His child. Although the world rejects you—maybe even your earthly father rejected you—God wants you to know that you have a heavenly Father who will never reject you. He will never turn His back on you. Jesus' final words to us as He walked this earth were, "Surely I am with you always, to the very end of the age" (Matthew 28:20). You are accepted, you are redeemed, you are His child, and you will always belong. This is God's household. If you're a follower of Christ, then you're in.

GOD WANTS TO USE YOUR REJECTION

Paul describes how this household of God's people is built "on the foundation of the apostles and the prophets, with Christ Himself as the chief cornerstone" (Ephesians 2:20). The most important part of this household is Christ. He is the cornerstone that bears the weight of it all. He is the cornerstone that gives guidance and direction to where everything else will be built.

Hopefully you are getting a little ahead of me by now. The title of this section probably gave it away, but I hope you're beginning to see the same revelation I saw in my journey. Think about it this way: **as Christ-followers, we are residents in a household that is built by, held up with, and guided by a stone that was initially labeled as rejection.** The beauty of Christ, His Church, and everything we stand for was established on a stone called rejection. Is this a beautiful story or what? God takes things that other people see as worthy of rejection and builds something beautiful.

**You are accepted, you are redeemed,
you are His child,
and you will always belong.**

Here's what I want you to see in this passage in Ephesians: there are two households mentioned as being built. On one hand, there is the household of the body of Christ that you and I are a part of. We're adopted into this house as children of God. That is mentioned here:

> You are no longer foreigners and strangers, but fellow citizens with God's people and also members of his household, built on the foundation of the apostles and prophets, with Christ Jesus himself as the chief cornerstone. In him the whole building is joined together and rises to become a holy temple in the Lord (Ephesians 2:19–21).

On the other hand, we have God building something up in us individually as well.

> And in Him you too are being built together to become a dwelling in which God lives by his Spirit (Ephesians 2:22).

Do you see it? He is building something in you too! Now, if rejection had to play a part in Jesus' life and, in turn, become the stone that the Church was built upon, what makes us think that rejection won't play a part in what God is building in us too? He's doing something in you as an individual, and He wants to use your rejection. If you have felt pain, if you have felt unloved, if you have felt abandoned, if you have felt the sorrows of this life, then guess what? That's the very thing that God might use to build something great in your life. God's desire is to use all of our hurts and pains for a purpose. He can take this cornerstone of rejection in your life and make it something that He can build beautifully upon.

But one thing is required before a stone can become a cornerstone. And that one thing is the fourth (and best) option.

God's desire is to use all of our hurts
and pains for a purpose.

THE BEST OPTION: LAY IT DOWN

Cornerstones were never meant to be hidden away, passed off, or carried around. They are meant to bear weight, not be a weight. What if your pain was never meant to weigh you down? Could the weight of your stone of rejection actually bear weight? Could it be that it was meant to bear the weight of the structure God is going to build in you? What God wants to build in your life could be built from a stone called rejection—one that you and everyone around you saw as a flaw or weakness. Like Jesus, the pain of your rejection could become the very cornerstone for what He is about to do in your life. However, with a cornerstone, one thing must occur before it can fulfill its true purpose: *it must be laid down.*

The moment a cornerstone is laid down, it becomes something that can be built upon. It becomes an object that bears weight. Until then, it is just a heavy weight to bear. I think you know that you cannot carry this weight any longer. Hopefully this book has exposed a stench behind the stone in your heart. And you know that God wants to do surgery on it. When you lay it down at the foot of the cross and choose to stand on it instead of carrying it, pain is placed in its rightful place. That place where you lay it down becomes the final resting place of pain.

LET'S GET PRACTICAL

Up until now, this book has been analogies, metaphors, stories, and motivating Scriptures. But I know what you're thinking— *What does this process look like day to day, Jon?* Because in a minute you have to put this book down and go to work or get the kids out of bed and off to school. Life does not pause or slow down just because we are doing heavy spiritual and emotional work.

It is really difficult to give specific steps to this journey. Every wilderness looks different, and not all pain, hardships, and struggles are created equal. To give a formula would be foolish and unwise. But we can look at practical examples in Scripture for reference and learning.

In the book of Acts, Paul and Barnabas are launched out into ministry by the church in Antioch. The two men go out and begin to preach the gospel in various places. What is the very first thing they encounter? Rejection.

> Then Paul and Barnabas answered them boldly: "We had to speak the word of God to you first. Since you reject it and do not consider yourselves worthy of eternal life, we now turn to the Gentiles" (Acts 13:46).

A few verses later, we learn of their reaction to the rejection they received: "So they shook the dust off their feet as a warning to them and went to Iconium" (v. 51). Jesus told His disciples to do the exact same thing in Matthew 10. After sending them out to heal the sick, raise the dead, and drive out demons, Jesus said, "If anyone will not welcome you or listen to your words, leave that home or town and shake the dust off your feet" (v. 14).

In both instances the people of God are told what to do when they receive rejection—shake it off. Acts 13 and Matthew 10 both use the same Greek word for "shake off." It is the Greek word *ektinassō*. The first translation of this word is 'to shake off so that something adhering shall fall.' This means that if you are not intentional about shaking it off, then you are going to carry it with you. But if you will shake off that which is trying to stick to you, it will fall. I believe this is what Isaac was trying to get Esau to understand when he told him, "You will shake his yoke from your neck" (Genesis 27:40). There is a way to overcome rejection, but you have to shake it off.

The second translation of *ektinassō* is 'to refuse to have any further dealings with it.' It is a refusal to engage. Once we begin to understand how to recognize rejection at its earliest stages, we can refuse to accept it. I choose to shake it off. Perhaps the most practical thing we can ever learn to do is recognize rejection before it clings to us. Before its seed takes root in us. The wisest thing to do is to build a guardrail at the top of the mountain instead of a hospital at the bottom of it.

Dealing with rejection is not a one-time event. Every day you will have the opportunity to be offended. This is what Jesus was explaining to His disciples. In every home or town they entered, dust would try to collect on them, and they were going to have to shake it off. Guess where dust ends up when you shake it off? Under your feet—the same place rejection belongs. In Romans 16:20, the apostle Paul writes, "The God of peace will soon crush Satan under your feet." My challenge to you is to lay it down. Declare that fear has no place in you. Insecurity has no place in you. Pain has no place in you. Rejection has no place in you. You're not going to carry it anymore. You're going to lay it down at the foot of the cross.

Another story in Scripture that gives us practical guidance in this process is the life of Joseph. He is one of my all-time favorites examples on the subject of overcoming rejection. Do you remember this story? If you didn't grow up in church, maybe you have seen or heard of the Broadway musical, *Joseph and the Amazing Technicolor Dreamcoat*. If you would like to read this story, it starts in Genesis 37. For now, though, I will give you a really quick overview. Joseph was the son of Israel (the man formerly known as Jacob). The Bible says that Joseph was his father's favorite child because he had been born to Israel in his old age. Israel gave Joseph a special robe, but this

I saw Jacob as good guy

Esau as bad guy

NOT TRUE

gift incited jealousy in Joseph's brothers. Here is the first sign of rejection in this story:

> When his brothers saw that their father loved him more than any of them, they hated him and could not speak a kind word to him (Genesis 37:4).

Joseph's brothers felt rejected by their father, and this seed of rejection produced the fruit of hatred. What happens when you hate someone? You reject them. Rejection is a cyclical process. It doesn't start with person A and end with person B. No, person B sends it back to person A as well as onward to person C and so forth. The process will keep going indefinitely until someone chooses to put a stop to it.

Genesis 37:5 says, "Joseph had a dream, and when he told it to his brothers, they hated him all the more." The dream was about the brothers bowing down to Joseph, and in retrospect, it was probably something the young man should have kept to himself. But he didn't, and the brothers' hatred exploded. When Joseph came to check on them in the fields, they tore off his robe and threw him into an empty cistern. They wanted to kill him but decided to sell him to slave traders instead. Obviously, the brothers couldn't tell Israel what they had done to his favorite child, so they put some blood on the robe, brought it to their father, and claimed, "We found this" (Genesis 37:32). Israel knew it was Joseph's robe and assumed that his son had been mauled to death by a wild animal. He had no idea his son was alive and on his way to slavery in Egypt.

I don't want to downplay your personal pain and rejection in any way, but what Joseph dealt with had to be some of the most difficult emotional pain a human has ever experienced. Rejected, abused, abandoned, and sold into slavery by his own family. How did Joseph respond to his incredibly difficult predicament? Let's find out.

When Joseph arrived in Egypt, he was purchased by Potiphar, Pharaoh's captain of the guard. How humiliating must that have been? But Genesis 39:2 says, "The Lord was with Joseph, so he succeeded in everything he did as he served in the home of his Egyptian master" (NLT). Even in the middle of humiliation, rejection, and pain, the Lord was with Joseph. God is with you in your rejection too. You may feel as though He has forgotten or abandoned you, but I promise He is still there.

What was Joseph's response to being sold into slavery? I would suggest that his first response was to serve.

> So Potiphar gave Joseph complete administrative responsibility over everything he owned. With Joseph there, he didn't worry about a thing—except what kind of food to eat! (Genesis 39:6 NLT).

Joseph proved himself so capable and trustworthy that even though he was a foreigner and a slave, he received leadership responsibilities. Considering the circumstances, things were going pretty well for the young man.

Cue the next problem. Genesis 39:7 tells us that Potiphar's wife became attracted to Joseph, and she tried to get him to sleep with her. Joseph rejected her advancements, and this rejection infuriated her. She lied to Potiphar, saying that Joseph had tried to sexually assault her. The next thing Joseph knew, he was sitting in prison. Rejected again.

If I were Joseph, I may have given up at this point. Imagine being in a prison in a foreign country with no hope of a trial. No one is going to give you a chance to prove your innocence, and you could literally be stuck behind bars for the rest of your life. Joseph could easily have become despondent, angry, or even suicidal. Here's what Scripture tells us, though:

But the Lord was with Joseph in the prison and showed him his faithful love. And the Lord made Joseph a favorite with the prison warden (Genesis 39:21 NLT).

Yet again, in the middle of rejection, the Lord was with Joseph and gave him great favor.

The warden had no more worries, because Joseph took care of everything. The Lord was with him and caused everything he did to succeed (Genesis 39:23 NLT).

No matter his circumstances, Joseph refused to give up. A common thread through his journey is the ever-present, ever-faithful, and ever-loving God. And the ability of a man to shake off pain and do the only thing that will ever get your mind off yourself and your problems—serve.

If anybody had an excuse to wallow in his rejection, it would have been Joseph. But look how his story ends. By keeping God first and His presence close, Joseph was able to lay down the stone of rejection that was far too heavy to carry and watch God build something beautiful upon it. It was the rejection he endured that became the cornerstone God would use to save the entire family of Israel.

Years later, after miraculously rising to power in Egypt and being reunited with his brothers, Joseph shared this wisdom:

You intended to harm me, but God intended it all for good. He brought me to this position so I could save the lives of many people (Genesis 50:20 NLT).

God can take whatever pain, whatever rejection, and whatever shame you carry and use it for His glory and for your good. You just have to stop carrying it, lay it at His feet, and let Him build something beautiful out of it. Joseph did not hide his pain. He

God can take whatever pain, whatever rejection, and whatever shame you carry and use it for His glory and for your good.

JESUS did too at The cross.

did not pass it off or carry it along either. No, Joseph laid it down and, in doing so, refused to drink from the cup of bitterness.

How do I know he wasn't bitter? Because when given the chance, he chose *not* to reject his brothers. If you're not familiar with the rest of Joseph's story, here is a brief recap. Joseph spent several years in prison, but then God used him to interpret Pharaoh's dreams. Pharaoh was so impressed with Joseph that he made the young man—a foreigner, a slave, and a prisoner—second in command over the entire land. When a severe famine devastated the region, Egypt still had plenty of food, thanks to Joseph's leadership. Soon, people from other nations started showing up in hopes of buying some of that food.

Joseph was in charge of the food distribution, and one day he noticed some familiar faces bowing in front of him. His brothers! The same guys who had rejected him, abused him, and sold him into slavery. Like many other people, the brothers had come to Egypt to buy food, but they had no idea that the man who had the power to accept or deny their request was the one they had treated so badly. Now remember, at this point, Joseph was an extremely powerful man. He could do whatever he wanted to whomever he wanted. So the moment he revealed his true identity to his brothers, they were terrified. Would he reject them as they had once rejected him?

What happened next shocked the brothers. Instead of exacting his revenge, Joseph began weeping! He said, "Don't be angry with yourselves for selling me to this place. It was God who sent me here ahead of you to preserve your lives" (Genesis 45:5 NLT). Joseph then invited his brothers to move to Egypt and promised to take care of them. The cycle of rejection was broken.

There may come a day when you, like Joseph, can stand upon the cornerstone of your rejection and realize, *God brought me to this position for a purpose.* Maybe you will use your experience with a troubled marriage to help others find healing for

God has us in this present situation for a purpose!

their relationships. Maybe your story of battling addiction will encourage others to break free from their own demons. What if God can use your past shame, abuse, and rejection to help others who are currently ashamed, abused, and rejected? Let me be very clear about something: I am not saying that God caused your pain just so you could have a good witnessing tool. That would make Him cruel and untrustworthy, both of which He is not. We do have an enemy who fits that description, though. First Peter 5:8 says the devil "prowls around like a roaring lion, looking for someone to devour." The devil wants to devour you with pain. But we have a heavenly Father who can take what the enemy tried to use to destroy our lives and make something beautiful instead. All we have to do is trust Him and lay down our pain.

Lay it down.

5

TIME TO TAKE GROUND

THE CHILDREN OF Israel crossed the Jordan River and received their circumcision. God rolled away the reproach of Egypt from them. The stench behind their stone was revealed, and God helped them fight the battle within.

Then something powerful happened:

> On the evening of the fourteenth day of the month, while camped at Gilgal on the plains of Jericho, the Israelites celebrated the Passover. The day after the Passover, that very day, they ate some of the produce of the land: unleavened bread and roasted grain. The manna stopped the day after they ate this food from the land; there was no longer any manna for the Israelites, but that year they ate the produce of Canaan (Joshua 5:10–12).

They ate of the fruit of the land. The dream they had heard their parents and grandparents talk about their entire lives finally came true. Seems like this is where you would roll the credits. Movie's over, everything ended happily ever after, and we can all go home. However, this isn't the end of the Israelites' story. Not even close! They escaped slavery, spent 40 years in the wilderness, fought the battle within on the banks of the Jordan, and now it was time to do something new—take ground. They had conquered half the battle (the battle within). Now it was time to fight the other half of the battle and take ground from the enemy.

We were never meant to sit back and enjoy the fruit of Jesus without using it to take ground from the enemy. Why would we fight and win the battle within and then not use that win to take ground from the enemy? God gave His people the Promised Land, but that didn't mean there wasn't going to be a battle. In fact, the very first thing they had to do in this "land flowing with milk and honey" was fight battles. Don't let the word *battle* scare you, by the way. Don't let it conjure up negative feelings like fear or distress. If you are a believer, then the word *battle* should bring one thought and one thought only into your mind—victory! **Life's toughest battles are where we find our greatest victories**.

The Israelites ate from the fruit of the land and then went straight to Jericho. Their first battle wasn't going to be a small one to get them warmed up. Jericho's walls were impenetrable. Joshua 6:1 says, "No one went out and no one came in. " The Israelites really only had two choices: go to battle and take territory in the land the Lord promised them or stay on the banks of the river and hunker down.

WAR IN THE TRENCHES

I love history, especially the history of major wars in modern times. I've long been fascinated by World War II, but a few years ago I began studying and researching World War I.

World War I, also known as the Great War, was a bizarre conflict, in that it was marked by some major changes in modern warfare. When looked back on in history, this war would become known as a war fought from the trenches. Trenches had been

**Life's toughest battles are where
we find our greatest victories.**

used in some ways in warfare for centuries (such as a castle moat), but in the context of these changes in warfare, they became a primary fortification and strategic necessity in WWI.

The definition of "battle" had changed. For centuries wars had been fought on horseback with swords, spears, knives, or gunpowder rifles that required long reloads. In the colonial era, battles were fought with rules of war. Each side faced the other and took turns fighting. Before that, castles were stormed and defended. But now the rules of war had changed, and the rule was, there are no rules. Also, the tools of war had changed. Soldiers were facing weapons of warfare that had never been seen before.

Weapons were more advanced than they had ever been. For the first time, airplanes were incorporated into combat, initially for observation purposes. By 1916, aircraft armed with machine guns were engaging in dogfights over the front lines.

The machine gun was improved and became a powerful mass killing tool. Consider this commentary on the battle of the Somme in July 1916:

> The initial advance was a disaster, as the six German divisions facing the advancing British mowed them down with their machine guns, killing or wounding some 60,000 men on the first day alone: the single heaviest day of casualties in British military history to that point.[15]

In 1915 the Germans unleashed poison chemical gas in attacks on Allied forces. The use of gas was adopted by both sides, at times being placed in artillery shells and shot into enemy trenches. Many of these weapons are banned today because of the terrible damage they cause. However, because of the close proximity of forces, the limited accuracy of delivery, the uncertain dispersal of the gas by the winds, and the rapid adoption of defensive tools such as gas masks, chemical weapons became limited in their effectiveness and use.

War in the seas changed as well. Submarines (known as U-boats by the Germans) were used by both sides from the beginning of the war, creating a new battlefield. This spurred the development of new technologies such as sonar to detect submarines as well as new weapons such as depth charges. The Germans' decision to start indiscriminate attacks on merchant vessels such as the Lusitania led to changes in British tactics, such as the use of convoys for protection.[16]

Tanks were also introduced during WWI. The Germans didn't have a comparable combat vehicle until near the end of the war, and this British invention, though hindered by slow speed, mechanical problems, and vulnerability to artillery, was able to cross trenches, barrel through fortifications, and resist machine-gun fire. The use of tanks contributed significantly to the Allied victory.

New rules and weapons of war created something of a stalemate in the early months of the war. Both sides were equipped for a typical mobility war, which could not be fought in these circumstances. Geography and politics played a part in this stalemate as well. The French had made a defense treaty with the Russians in 1895. This meant the Germans would have to face opposition on two fronts. Their primary goal was to conquer Europe, so their thrust was to take the Western Front from the French and Allied forces. However, their army was sandwiched between Russia and the North Sea. They had to maintain reinforced defenses when they could not advance unilaterally. The trench system was developed to deal with this stalemate:

In the wake of the Battle of the Marne—during which Allied troops halted the steady German push through Belgium and France that had proceeded over the first month of World

War I—a conflict both sides had expected to be short and decisive turns longer and bloodier, as Allied and German forces begin digging the first trenches on the Western Front on September 15, 1914.

The trench system on the Western Front in World War I—fixed from the winter of 1914 to the spring of 1918—eventually stretched from the North Sea coast of Belgium southward through France, with a bulge outwards to contain the much-contested Ypres salient. Running in front of such French towns as Soissons, Reims, Verdun, St. Mihiel and Nancy, the system finally reached its southernmost point in Alsace, at the Swiss border. In total the trenches built during World War I, laid end-to-end, would stretch some 35,000 miles—12,000 of those miles occupied by the Allies, and the rest by the Central Powers.[17]

The bloodshed slowed, but so did the advancement. Troops on both sides were dug in, hiding, and kept from taking any ground from the enemy. **What was meant to be a place of safety became their sanctuary.** Perhaps at times this describes us too. The enemy has attacked us with weapons we have never faced before—new weapons that we do not know how to defend against. New challenges, new difficulties, new mindsets, new emotions, new temptations, or new circumstances. Instead of advancing to take ground from the enemy, we find ourselves digging trenches for us to hide in. The problem with trenches in World War I is that they would go from being places of safety and security to places of stench and death.

THE SILENT KILLERS

It was safety the soldiers sought in the trenches. A moment away from the bullets and bloodshed. Shrapnel from mortars, grenades and, above all, artillery projectile bombs, or shells, would account for an estimated 60 percent of the 9.7 million military fatalities of World War I.[18] So the trenches is where they went. What they did not know is that lurking in these disease-infested trenches were many silent killers. These killers would account for most of the casualties not accounted for in the statistic above.

It was fear that drove troops to the trenches. And fear is what met them in the trenches as well. The mental and emotional weight on every soldier was extreme. Every sound in the night might be your end. Every flash of movement in the trench could be the enemy coming to kill you. Every bullet flying over your head might have your name on it. Every incoming mortar round might reap destruction on you and your comrades next to you.

Along with new weapons and new tactics of war came a new type of injury. The barrages of artillery fire and explosions in the trenches and constant sniper fire gave rise to a term first coined in World War I: *shell shock*. This word first appeared in the British medical journal *The Lancet* in February 1915, only six months after the commencement of the war.[19] Soldiers suffered from the concussive effects of shells and explosions (what we would today call traumatic brain injury, or TBI) as well as emotional distress, even among some who were not affected as directly physically (what we would today call PTSD). Unfortunately, medical and psychological knowledge back then was not adequate to distinguish between the two, and troops with PTSD were more likely to be sent back to the front lines.[20] As a result, the trenches of the front line became a place of extreme trauma and paranoia. And in many documented cases, paranoia would lead to confusion. In some instances, troops would shoot at their own comrades because of the confusion.

I think we can relate to this type of behavior in our own lives. Perhaps no one is firing bullets at us, but our jobs, families, responsibilities, and strains have a way of firing some pretty nasty stress and worry our way. I know that when I feel stressed and pushed too far, I can end up firing at the ones I love the most. I lose my temper and raise my voice at my kids. I treat friends as enemies. When you are in the middle of battle, the stressful trenches of your job, self-imposed isolation, or a difficult season of life, it's easy to fire at family and friends without even realizing that you are doing it.

I think this is the enemy's strategy with us many times. It might not be the obvious bullets that take us down. You may never get addicted to heavy drugs or pornography, cheat on your spouse, or physically injure another person. Perhaps our greatest vulnerabilities are in the places we would never think to look. The place of greatest trauma might not be on the battle-field but in the trenches—in the very places where you're trying to avoid the enemy's attacks. For many of us, we might get attacked by more subtle and silent killers. We might suffer from ailments like complacency, sadness, depression, shame, or guilt. A problem doesn't have to be dramatic in order to be dangerous.

The trenches of World War I helped protect soldiers from external weapons. But the trenches were also infested with enemies that attacked from the inside out. WWI trenches were dirty, smelly, and riddled with sickness, rats, human waste, decomposing bodies, and more. Diseases such as influenza, typhoid fever, and even malaria were birthed in the trenches. (Malaria alone was responsible for hundreds of thousands of hospitalizations and tens of thousands of deaths.)[21]

Various pests and physical ailments affected the troops. Attracted and nourished by the food and waste in the trenches, rats spread disease. Lice, which infested a large number of soldiers, caused *trench fever*, which plagued the troops with headaches, fevers, and muscle pain. WWI saw a major outbreak of a dangerous frostbite-like condition known as *trench foot*,

The place of greatest trauma might not be
on the battlefield but in the trenches

caused by the persistently cold, damp conditions. In extreme cases trench foot could lead to gangrene or even amputation.[22]

Trench foot affected soldiers' ability to walk. Like those soldiers, if we are not careful, the trenches we barricade ourselves in can affect our walk with Christ. The apostle Paul wrote, "Therefore, as you received Christ Jesus the Lord, so walk in him" (Colossians 2:6 ESV). If we can't walk with Christ, we certainly cannot advance to take ground from the enemy. Your walk will determine your win.

The very trenches that were dug to bring safety were laced with parasites at every turn that could kill you from the inside out. What I am suggesting to you today is that we need to make a continual scan of our internal selves. Allow God to examine your heart to ensure you are not carrying hurt, pain, or spiritual parasites that could become the silent killer of your soul.

Life in the trenches was the catalyst for yet another physical problem: trench mouth. This painful disease of the gums and mouth tissue was brought on by exhaustion, emotional stress, and poor health conditions, such as deficient diets, tobacco use, insufficient rest, and poor oral hygiene. The trench you find yourself in today can have an effect on your mouth as well. Have you ever been around someone who is constantly negative? Or perhaps they are constantly talking down to others, criticizing others, or gossiping about others. According to Proverbs 18:21, "The tongue has the power of life and death." Yet another slow and silent killer in the trenches is the effect it has on our mouth.

If we look closely enough at our own lives, we can find that our own trenches are laced with silent killers. Our trenches may not carry physical sicknesses, but they are riddled with mental and spiritual disease. We can find toxic mindsets lingering in our trenches, and bitterness and unforgiveness can be found doing great damage.

Defensive

TROOPS CANNOT TRIUMPH IN THE TRENCHES

The deeper I dove into the study and research of the trenches of World War I, the more symbolism and analogies I saw in the lives of believers. Troops could not triumph in the trenches, and neither can we. We cannot fight for our marriages, kids, finances, or the advancement of God's kingdom if the fear of new weapons and challenges forces us to dig a hole and hide in it. Trenches stop us from taking ground back from the enemy.

I'm convinced that many times the devil doesn't even need to attack us, because we are busy killing each other in the trenches of hateful words, wrong thinking, unforgiveness, bitterness, or the ever-infectious social media. We are catching silent yet deadly diseases in our spirits that slowly but surely kill us from the inside out. You may think I'm being a little melodramatic with the intensity of my writing, but let me remind you of what Paul warned the church of Ephesus:

> For we are not fighting against flesh-and-blood enemies, but against evil rulers and authorities of the unseen world, against mighty powers in this dark world, and against evil spirits in the heavenly places (Ephesians 6:12).

Maybe you have never thought about being in a spiritual war. Or perhaps you have thought about it, and you've dug a trench to try to hide from it. The only good thing for the soldiers in World War I was that their enemies were hiding in trenches too. But our enemy doesn't hide in a trench. John 10:10 says, "The thief comes only to steal and kill and destroy." The devil is not hiding from you; instead, he is walking from trench to trench, looking for people whom he can destroy.

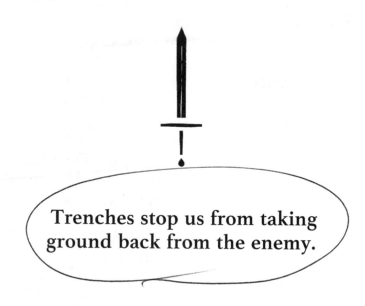

When I think of people hiding in trenches, I think of Gideon in the Bible. Remember this guy? You may have heard sermons about Gideon's mighty victory, but let's back up to the beginning of his story. When we are first introduced to Gideon, the Israelites are in deep distress. The opening verses of Judges 6 explain the reason why:

> The Israelites did evil in the Lord's sight. So the Lord handed them over to the Midianites for seven years. The Midianites were so cruel that the Israelites made hiding places for themselves in the mountains, caves, and strongholds. . . . Israel was reduced to starvation by the Midianites (vv. 1–2, 6 NLT).

This wasn't the first time the people of God "did evil in the Lord's sight," and sadly, it wouldn't be the last. The problem started when Joshua died. Sure, the Israelites had struggled to trust and obey God throughout their wilderness journey, and they even had some setbacks when conquering the Promised Land. But they always had strong leaders such as Moses and Joshua to guide them back to the right path. Judges 2:7 says, "The Israelites served the Lord throughout the lifetime of Joshua and the leaders who outlived him—those who had seen all the great things the Lord had done for Israel" (NLT).

So what happened after Joshua's death? "Another generation grew up who did not acknowledge the Lord or remember the mighty things he had done for Israel" (Judges 2:10 NLT). Instead of serving the one true God as their ancestors did, the Israelites began worshipping the false gods of the surrounding nations. They removed themselves from God's blessing and protection. Then everything went horribly wrong. Enemy nations began to oppress the Israelites, and their new "gods" didn't do anything to help them! The Israelites found themselves in such a dire predicament that they cried out for God's help. Judges 2:16

says, "The Lord raised up judges to rescue the Israelites from their attackers" (NLT). These leaders helped God's people defeat their enemies and break free from oppression. It never lasted long, though.

> But when the judge died, the people returned to their corrupt ways, behaving worse than those who had lived before them. They went after other gods, serving and worshiping them. And they refused to give up their evil practices and stubborn ways (Judges 2:19 NLT).

When we meet Gideon in Judges 6, the Israelites have gotten themselves into terrible trouble yet again. They are on the verge of being wiped out by the Midianites, and only a swift act of divine intervention will save them. The following is God's response:

> Then the angel of the Lord came and sat beneath the great tree at Ophrah, which belonged to Joash of the clan of Abiezer. Gideon son of Joash was threshing wheat at the bottom of a winepress to hide the grain from the Midianites. The angel of the Lord appeared to him and said, "Mighty hero, the Lord is with you!" (Judges 6:11–12 NLT).

Wait a minute. Does God have the right person? He calls Gideon a "mighty hero," but this man isn't doing anything heroic. In fact, he's doing something really ordinary (just not in an ordinary place). In case you aren't familiar with farming terminology, threshing is a method used to separate grain from the stalk by beating it against a hard surface. Once separated, the grain is then winnowed; it is thrown into the air, and the wind separates the grain from any remaining chaff. The entire process usually takes place on a designated threshing floor, but for Gideon, that wasn't an option. He had to hide every scrap of food from the Midianites, so he chose a hiding place in which the enemy hopefully wouldn't think to look. The winepress wasn't a great place to thresh wheat, but it would keep Gideon alive for another day. In a land full of suffering, the winepress was Gideon's trench.

Let's jump back to World War I for just a moment. The distance between opposing trenches was sometimes very short. It could be as few as 50–250 yards. Think about that. Soldiers were less than a quarter of a mile away from their enemy, but they remained stuck in place for almost four years. What held them back? A terrifying area known as "no man's land." No one who entered this land came back to tell about it (hence the name). This area was filled with land mines, barbed wire, machine guns, sniper fire, and constant mortar fire. To make matters even worse, the terrain was so difficult that no horse, tank, or machinery could get through it. No matter how the soldiers looked at it, the gap seemed insurmountable.

Gideon wasn't a soldier, but he was definitely familiar with insurmountable problems. His people were starving and suffering, and the Midianites didn't show any signs of backing down. Like the soldiers in WWI, the Israelites were living in the trenches, barely surviving and full of despair. So what makes Gideon leave the winepress and venture in his own no man's land? I'll unpack that more in the following sections, but the simple answer is this: God gives him the courage to take the land back from the enemy. God isn't okay with Gideon staying in his trench, and He isn't okay with you staying in yours either.

FIRST IMPARTATION

The first impartation God gives Gideon is a new name for the battlefield.

The angel of the Lord appeared to him and said, "Mighty hero, the Lord is with you!" (Judges 6:12 NLT).

Now, if God showed up and called me a "mighty hero," I would be pretty excited. After all, if God says it, then it has to be true! But Gideon's response is less than enthusiastic.

"Sir," Gideon replied, "if the Lord is with us, why has all this happened to us? And where are the miracles our ancestors told us about? Didn't they say, 'The Lord brought us up out of Egypt'? But now the Lord has abandoned us and handed us over the Midianites" (Judges 6:13 NLT).

Frustration. Humiliation. Exhaustion. Trench living has worn the Israelites down, and Gideon is no exception. So when God shows up, this man has some burning questions for Him. *If You rescued our ancestors, then why haven't You rescued us? Where have You been? Do You even care?*

Gideon struggles to have faith, both in God and in himself. In verse 15, he further objects, "How can I rescue Israel? My clan is the weakest in the whole tribe of Manasseh, and I am the least in my entire family!" (NLT). Know what that sounds like to me? Rejection. In the third chapter of this book, I talked about how the seeds of rejection grow best in the soil of fear. The Israelites have lived in a constant state of fear for seven years, so I don't think it should surprise us that Gideon has rejection issues. It's definitely not a surprise to God. That's why He begins the interaction in verse 12 by giving Gideon a new name. With this new name comes a new identity. No longer is Gideon rejected, forgotten, and worthless. Instead, he is chosen, remembered, and loved.

At the end of verse 16, God tells Gideon, "You will destroy the Midianites as if you were fighting against one man" (NLT).

While this does apply to the physical skirmish between Israel and Midian, I also believe it describes the battle Gideon has to fight on the inside. "As if you were fighting against one man." Perhaps that "one man" is the greatest enemy Gideon will ever fight—the enemy named rejection.

SECOND IMPARTATION

The second impartation God gives Gideon is boldness.

> Then the Lord turned to him and said, "Go with the strength you have, and rescue Israel from the Midianites. I am sending you!" (Judges 6:14 NLT).

Gideon certainly doesn't see himself as a hero, but a tiny seed of boldness is planted in his heart. He tells God, "If you are truly going to help me, show me a sign to prove that it is really the Lord speaking to me" (v. 17 NLT). God gives Gideon the requested sign, and the seed of boldness begins to take root.

After he summons warriors from several Israelite tribes, Gideon's self-doubt starts to return. Instead of running back to the winepress, though, he regains his composure and asks the Lord for another sign. Then, in chapter 7, Gideon boldly obeys God's directive to reduce the size of Israel's army by over 90 percent. The man we first met hiding in the winepress becomes so bold that when the leaders of a town refuse to give his soldiers some food, Gideon replies, "I will return and tear your flesh with the thorns and briers from the wilderness" (Judges 8:7 NLT). What a transformation!

When God first appears to Gideon, He gives this promise: "I will be with you, and you will strike down all the Midianites, leaving none alive" (Judges 6:16). Remember, Gideon is still hiding in the winepress at this point. He's probably thinking,

Me? Me and what army? The Israelites have been praying for a breakthrough, but Gideon has a hard time believing that God wants him to play a major role in it.

There are times in life when God shows up in a miraculous way and brings a breakthrough that you never saw coming. You didn't do anything to make it happen. Salvation is one example. It's the greatest breakthrough that's ever been done. There's nothing you can do to buy or earn your way into God's favor. It's a totally free gift, and, best of all, it's available to everyone.

But there are other times in life when a breakthrough requires a break of sweat. These are the times when God asks you to pony up and do the work. You may think, *If God is all-powerful, why can't He just handle my problems for me?* It is true that God is all-powerful, but He's also all-knowing. If He is asking you to do the work, then He knows that being a part of the process is essential to your spiritual and emotional growth. The Israelites are going to have a breakthrough, but Gideon is going to have to break a sweat.

Is God asking you to break a sweat today? Maybe your difficulty is in the area of finances. Could God miraculously cancel your debt? Yes, He could do that. Maybe one day you will win the lottery, or you will open your mailbox and find a check inside for the exact amount needed to pay all your bills. That would be awesome, wouldn't it? But it's much more likely that God will help you get out of debt by asking you to break a sweat. Little by little, day by day, ramen noodle by ramen noodle, you will do whatever you have to do to chip your way out of debt.

Maybe your problem is unforgiveness. You know you need to release that person who hurt you, whether it was last week or 10 years ago. It would be so much easier if God would just erase that person from your memory (or the earth), but chances are, He's not going to do that. Instead, you're going to have to work to forgive that person. You're going to have to break a sweat and consciously choose forgiveness today and tomorrow and for the rest of your life.

Many people struggle with difficulties in their marriage. Do you know what you may have to do? You may have to break a sweat and actually date your spouse again. Court them the way you courted them back at the beginning of your relationship—before the house, before the kids, and before all the messy details. Perhaps the problem isn't your spouse but your dead-beat boss. Sure, you could quit your job, but most people need a steady income. That means you may have to break a sweat and serve your boss yet another day. I'll let you in on a secret I've learned while working in the ministry: God often asks us to serve someone else's vision before He will bring ours to fruition.

I'm reminded of the story in Mark 2, when some men bring their paralyzed friend to see Jesus. They carry him to the house where the Lord is preaching, but when they arrive, they can't get through the mass of people. They could have given up and said, "Sorry man, we tried. Jesus is just too busy." But they don't give up. Verse 4 says, "When they could not come near Him because of the crowd, they uncovered the roof where He was. So when they had broken through, they let down the bed on which the paralytic was lying" (NKJV). Jesus is impressed by their faith, and He heals the paralyzed man.

When is the breakthrough in this story? Most of us would say it is the moment when Jesus tells the paralyzed man, "Take your mat and go home" (v. 11). However, this healing breakthrough comes only after his friends' literal breakthrough on the roof. In stubbornness and determination (and probably to the chagrin of the homeowner), they open a hole big enough to lower the paralyzed man in front of Jesus. If they hadn't broken a sweat, their friend would never have experienced his breakthrough.

**God often asks us to serve someone else's
vision before He will bring ours to fruition.**

You hear people say this all the time: "I just can't catch a break." Imagine the paralyzed man. His friends carry him up to the house, and then they just stop. There's no room. I can picture this man looking up at his friends and saying, "Well guys, you gave it your best shot. It just wasn't my day. Thank you for trying." But these friends examine the house, and after taking a look at the roof, say to each other, "Think we can do it? It's make or break. Let's get this guy up there. Let's make our own story. Let's break through this thing to get this guy his breakthrough." I'm sure the paralyzed man was so thankful that they didn't bail on his breakthrough. That they didn't give up. He may not have been able to achieve his breakthrough on his own, but he surrounded himself with people who said, "We're going to help you get your breakthrough, and we're willing to break a sweat."

It's like the woman who had the issue of bleeding for 12 years (see Matthew 9:20–22 and Mark 5:25–30). When was her breakthrough? Was it the moment when she touched the hem of Jesus' garment and was healed because of her faith? Or was it when she decided to risk everything, push through the crowd, and take those first steps toward the Healer? There was a spiritual breakthrough before the physical breakthrough ever happened. There was a sweat. There was a desire. There was faith.

It's like in 1 Samuel 1, when Hannah wanted to have a baby but was unable to conceive. The pain of an empty womb was made worse by the taunts of her husband's other wife, who did have children. Hannah needed a breakthrough. Verse 10 says, "In her deep anguish Hannah prayed to the Lord, weeping bitterly." This woman poured out her soul (see v. 15). God heard Hannah's desperate plea and gave her a child. It's easy to assume her breakthrough came the moment she became pregnant, but I believe it was when she cried out to God.

Michele and I had a very similar story early in our marriage. We waited several years to have children. Then when we started trying to have a family, we had trouble getting pregnant. We went to specialists and spent thousands of dollars on procedures, medications, and shots. But we just couldn't get pregnant. One night I sat down at my computer and typed out a letter to God. It was a way for me to process my thoughts in an organized and thoughtful manner. Like Hannah, I poured out my soul. The doctor had said we were doing everything medically possible. We needed a divine breakthrough, and before giving up, I was going to break a sweat. A short time later, we received word that we were pregnant with our daughter, Corey. God answered our prayers! But our breakthrough didn't happen when we had our first positive pregnancy test or even when the doctor's office called to confirm. Our breakthrough came at a keyboard, where I broke a sweat and poured out my heart to an ever-listening God.

Your breakthrough could be just around the corner, but you have to take those first steps out of the trench. God gave Gideon the boldness to get out of the winepress and achieve his destiny. May this be the day God imparts the same boldness to you! You don't have to be perfect or know all the answers to all the questions. Go with the strength you have. Go with the bank account you have. Go with the marriage and kids you have. Go with the education and skills you have. God declares He is with you. You no longer need the trench.

THIRD IMPARTATION

The third impartation God gives Gideon is peace. Have you ever known that God told you to do something, but even though you wanted to obey, you felt paralyzed by fear, shame, doubt, or insecurity? If so, you aren't alone. God directly confronts fear time and time again in Gideon's story, and I think He is confronting it in our stories as well. When the Lord appears on the scene in Judges 6, He tells Gideon, "Go in the strength you have" (v. 14). Gideon's fear is apparent as he tries to disqualify himself by claiming to be the weakest person from the weakest clan. What is he really saying? *I'm scared. I'm fearful.* God doesn't let Gideon off the hook, though. Instead, the Lord replies, "I will be with you, and you will strike down all the Midianites, leaving none alive" (v. 16).

I believe Gideon has an internal tug-of-war at this point. His fear screams that everything about this interaction is wrong. There's no way a nobody like him could ever do anything for God—certainly not something as massively important as saving the people of Israel. And yet God is standing right in front of him saying, "You can do this. I will be with you the entire time, and you will be victorious." Fear makes Gideon want to run away, but he decides to take a giant leap of faith and asks God for a sign—"Please do not go away until I come back and bring my offering and sit it before you" (Judges 6:18).

Gideon brings an offering of a young goat and unleavened bread, and the angel of the Lord consumes both by fire. Then Gideon has a moment of panic.

> When Gideon realized that it was the angel of the Lord, he exclaimed, "Alas, Sovereign Lord! I have seen the angel of the Lord face to face!" (Judges 6:22).

I can just imagine the thoughts going through Gideon's mind— *That's it. I'm a dead man. I should have just kept threshing the wheat and never looked up.* Instead of scolding the man for his fear, though, God brings comfort and encouragement: "Peace! Do not be afraid. You are not going to die" (v. 23). I believe these words transform Gideon's perception of God. Remember, back in verse 13, he had lamented, "The Lord has abandoned us." It's hard to trust someone who you think has abandoned you. Verse 24 is a crucial turning point for Gideon:

> Gideon built an altar to the Lord there and named it Yahweh-Shalom (which means "the Lord is peace") (NLT).

Outwardly, nothing has changed. The Midianites are still oppressing God's people. But Gideon now knows something new. Peace isn't a feeling dependent upon circumstances. Peace comes from the Lord, and when you have Him, you don't have to be afraid.

One of the things I love about God in the story of Gideon is His never-ending patience. At the end of Judges 6, Gideon summons troops from the tribes of Manasseh, Asher, Zebulun, and Naphtali. They all show up! You might expect Gideon to be feeling pretty good about himself at this point. After all, he didn't know if anyone was going to answer the call to arms or not. However, even after the men arrive, Gideon still has some self-doubt. What makes him qualified to lead these soldiers? Will they listen to him? Is God absolutely sure that Gideon is the right guy?

> Gideon said to God, "If you will save Israel by my hand as you have promised— look, I will place a wool fleece on the threshing floor. If there is dew only on the fleece and all the ground is dry, then I will know that you will save Israel by my hand, as you said." And that is what happened. Gideon rose early the next day; he squeezed the fleece and wrung out the dew—a bowlful of water.
>
> Then Gideon said to God, "Do not be angry with me. Let me make just one more request. Allow me one more test with the fleece, but this time make the fleece dry and let the ground be covered with dew." That night God did so. Only the fleece was dry; all the ground was covered with dew (vv. 36–40).

Peace isn't a feeling dependent
upon circumstances. Peace comes
from the Lord, and when you have Him,
you don't have to be afraid.

Through the fleece and the dew, God gives Gideon the peace he needs to do the work God has called him to do.

In Judges 7, Gideon's peace is put to the test when God tells him that Israel's army is too big.

> The Lord said to Gideon, "You have too many men. I cannot deliver Midian into their hands, or Israel would boast against me, 'My own strength has saved me.' Now announce to the army, 'Anyone who trembles with fear may turn back and leave Mount Gilead.'" So twenty-two thousand men left, while ten thousand remained (vv. 2–3).

With just one announcement, over two-thirds of the army disappears. I believe God's purpose here is two-fold. He wants to prevent pride from developing in the future, but He also wants to eradicate fear in the present. That's why God tells Gideon to send home "anyone who trembles with fear." Fear is not allowed to have any place in Israel's camp.

God continues whittling down Israel's army until only 300 men remain. He says, "With the three hundred men . . . I will save you and give the Midianites into your hands" (Judges 7:7). It is finally time for Gideon to lead Israel to victory over the enemy. There's still one place of fear remaining, though.

> During that night the Lord said to Gideon, "Get up, go down against the camp, because I am going to give it into your hands. If you are afraid to attack, go down to the camp with your servant Purah and listen to what they are saying. Afterward, you will be encouraged to attack the camp" (Judges 7:9–11).

Did you see what God said? "If you're afraid to attack, go down to the camp." What does Gideon do? He takes his servant and goes down to the camp. What does that tell us? Fear still exists. God wants to get every last ounce of fear out of Gideon before the battle begins.

> Gideon arrived just as a man was telling a friend his dream. "I had a dream," he was saying. "A round loaf of barley bread came tumbling into the Midianite camp. It struck the tent with such force that the tent overturned and collapsed."
>
> His friend responded, "This can be nothing other than the sword of Gideon son of Joash, the Israelite. God has given the Midianites and the whole camp into his hands" (Judges 7:13–14).

God said Gideon would be encouraged by what he heard, and as always, God was right! Verse 15 says, "When Gideon heard the dream and its interpretation, he bowed down and worshiped." The physical battle has not yet taken place, but the war in Gideon's heart is over. Fear is gone. The remainder of verse 15 says, "He returned to the camp of Israel and called out, 'Get up! The Lord has given the Midianite camp into your hands.'"

FOURTH IMPARTATION

The fourth impartation God gives Gideon is insulation. Up until this point Gideon has felt nothing but isolation. God wants Gideon to know, "You no longer need to feel isolated and alone. I am here to insulate you and be with you in this battle."

> The Lord said to him, "I will be with you. And you will destroy the Midianites as if you were fighting against one man" (Judges 6:16 NLT).

I will be with you. These five words are enough to make Gideon climb out of the winepress and ask for a sign. Sometimes it's enough to know that you're not by yourself.

Throughout Scripture we find God telling His people, "I am with you." Sometimes He gives them details about the battle they will be facing; other times, He does not. Either way, God offers His people the comfort of His presence. Here are just three examples:

- God appears to Moses through a burning bush and tells him to lead the people of Israel out of slavery in Egypt. When Moses objects, God replies, "I will be with you" (Exodus 3:12).
- After Moses' death, God commissions Joshua to lead the Israelites. He promises, "As I was with Moses, so I will be with you; I will never leave you nor forsake you" (Joshua 1:5).
- The angel Gabriel appears to Mary to tell her that she is going to give birth to a son. His first words are, "Greetings, you who are highly favored! The Lord is with you" (Luke 1:28).

Gideon, Moses, Joshua, and Mary were not alone. You are not alone either. God says the same thing to you that He said to them—"I am with you." Remember Jesus' last words on this earth:

And surely I am with you always, to the very end of the age (Matthew 28:20).

One of the many names for God in the Bible is *Yahweh Shammah,* and it means "the Lord is there" (Ezekiel 48:35). God is there in your situation. He's there in your predicament. He's there in your pain.

Gideon's courage to step out of the trench and on to the battlefield inspires others to follow. Watch what it says in Judges 6:33–35:

Soon afterward the armies of Midian, Amalek, and the people of the east formed an alliance against Israel and crossed the Jordan, camping in the valley of Jezreel. Then the Spirit of the Lord clothed Gideon with power. He blew a ram's horn as a call to arms, and the men of the clan of Abiezer came to him. He also sent messengers throughout Manasseh, Asher, Zebulun, and Naphtali, summoning their warriors, and all of them responded (NLT).

Gideon rises above his rejection, fear, and isolation. I believe you can do the same thing. Choose today to step out of your trench and on to the battlefield.

6

THE WEAPON FOR WAR

YOU MAY BE ready to face your Jericho now, or you may still be fighting the battle within. Either way, there will come a day when you have to face a hardship in this fallen world. As a pastor, I frequently get the question, "Why did this happen?" Sometimes the answer is fairly obvious, but much of the time it isn't. I often have to shake my head and answer, "I'm sorry, but I don't know." What I do know is this: no matter who you are, battles are ahead. I don't say this to scare you but to prepare you. Whether the issue will involve your career, family, health, finances, or something else, you can start getting ready today in order to win the battle tomorrow.

When we left Gideon in the last chapter, he was ready to lead his men to victory. As you read the following verses, notice the three distinct items that the Israelite troops use in battle. I believe this is a clear picture of what we must carry into our battlefield to win the victory.

Gideon and the hundred men with him reached the edge of the camp at the beginning of the middle watch, just after they had changed the guard. They blew their trumpets and broke the jars that were in their hands. The three companies blew the trumpets and smashed the jars. Grasping the torches in their left hands and holding in their right hands the trumpets they were to blow, they shouted, "A sword for the Lord and for Gideon!" While each man held his position around the camp, all the Midianites ran, crying out as they fled. When the three hundred trumpets sounded, the Lord caused the men throughout the camp to turn on each other with their swords (Judges 7:19–22).

THE TORCH

Jesus said, "I have come into the world as a light, so that no one who believes in me should stay in darkness" (John 12:46). What is the light—the torch—that we carry with us? The answer is Jesus. Very simply put, you have to carry Christ into your battle. He is the only thing in you that's worth anything. When the Israelites carried their torches into battle, it was symbolic of us carrying Christ into ours.

The gospel of John begins with these words about Jesus:

In the beginning was the Word, and the Word was with God, and the Word was God. He was with God in the beginning. Through him all things were made; without him nothing was made that has been made. In him was life, and that life was the light of all mankind. The light shines in the darkness, and the darkness has not overcome it (John 1:1–5).

This Word is the same word spoken of in Psalm 119:105:

Your word is a lamp for my feet,
 a light on my path.

Jesus, the Word, is the light who guides our steps and invades the darkness. You must carry this torch into your battles. If you do not have the light of Christ with you, then you are just

You have to carry Christ into your battle.
He is the only thing in you
that's worth anything.

wandering around in the darkness. You don't even know where the battle is.

THE TRUMPET

Judges 7:20 says, "Grasping the torches in their left hands and holding in their right hands the trumpets they were to blow." Now, don't panic; you don't need to go out and buy a trumpet. And you don't have to bring your shofar to church. But the trumpet symbolizes something in the text.

Back in Gideon's day, people only blew the trumpet for one of three reasons. The first reason was to summon everyone to corporate prayer. The second reason was to summon people to corporate worship. The third reason was to summon people to corporate battle. Two words are present in all three scenarios—*summon* and *corporate*. So what is the common denominator? Unity.

When the body of Christ comes together in unity, something powerful happens. Breakthrough comes. Why? Because God is a God of unity. David wrote in Psalm 133:

> How good and pleasant it is
>> when God's people live together in unity!
> It is like precious oil poured on the head,
>> running down on the beard,
> running down on Aaron's beard,
>> down on the collar of his robe.
> It is as if the dew of Hermon
>> were falling on Mount Zion.
> For there the Lord bestows his blessing,
>> even life forevermore.

Think about this: when Jesus prayed for us in John 17, He could have prayed for any number of traits. He could have prayed for strength, courage, passion, or good behavior. Instead, however, Jesus prayed for something else.

> I pray also for those who will believe in me through their message, **that all of them may be one,** Father, just as you are in me and I am in you. May they also be in us so that the world may believe that you have sent me (vv. 20–21, bold added).

Gideon's army conquered because they were united. Look again at Judges 7:22. It says, "When the 300 trumpets sounded, the Lord caused the men throughout the camp to turn on each other with their swords." For 300 trumpets to sound together, there had to be unity.

The opposite of unity is disunity. Matthew 12:25 presents to us the impact of disunity: "Every kingdom divided against itself will be ruined, and every city or household divided against itself will not stand." The Israelites carried a torch and a trumpet, but what won them the battle was the thing that was in the enemy's hands. The Midianites had swords. Most people would select a sword over a torch or a trumpet as their weapon of choice. But the Midianites never used their swords against the Israelites; instead, they used them on each other! Then they ran away (see Judges 7:23). Disunity cost the Midianites everything.

THE TONGUE

Perhaps the greatest weapon wielded on any battlefield is not a sword, a gun, or even a bomb. The greatest weapon may be the human tongue. Proverbs 18:21 says, "The tongue has the power of life and death." I believe that the army of Israel ultimately won with the power of the tongue. You can see the moment of breakthrough in the text:

They shouted, "A sword for the Lord and for Gideon!" While each man held his position around the camp, all the Midianites ran, crying out as they fled (Judges 7:20–21)

It was not swords and strength that sent the enemy running but faith and shouts of praise. We see it time and time again in Scripture. Praise is a weapon of mass destruction to your enemies. Rising above your circumstances and giving praise to your God is the very thing that's going to cause the breakthrough in your life.

I began this book by talking about the children of Israel and their entrance into the Promised Land. They escaped slavery, wandered in the wilderness, and crossed the Jordan River at flood stage. They fought the battle within and circumcised themselves to be reminded of their covenant with God. God told them, "Today I have rolled back the reproach of Egypt from you" (Joshua 5:9). Now they were ready for their very first battle with a physical enemy—Jericho. We already know that Jericho's walls fall down and the Israelites conquer the city. Here's something else we need to know: we are victorious too.

For everyone born of God overcomes the world. This is the victory that has overcome the world, even our faith. Who is it that overcomes the world? Only the one who believes that Jesus is the Son of God (1 John 5:4–5).

The children of Israel walked into the Promised Land knowing that God had already given them that territory. They still had to fight, though. If you are a child of God, you have a Promised Land, and you need to fight for it.

Let's go to the beginning phases of the Jericho fight and see how we should approach our battles.

Rising above your circumstances and giving praise to your God is the very thing that's going to cause the breakthrough in your life.

Joshua got up early the next morning and the priests took up the ark of the Lord. The seven priests carrying the seven trumpets went forward, marching before the ark of the Lord and blowing the trumpets. The armed men went ahead of them and the rear guard followed the ark of the Lord, while the trumpets kept sounding. So on the second day they marched around the city once and returned to the camp. They did this for six days (Joshua 6:12–14).

The ark of the covenant represented the very presence of God, and it was there on the battlefield with them. They dared not go to war without it. God had given Moses these instructions:

Place the cover on top of the ark and put in the ark the tablets of the covenant law that I will give you. There, above the cover between the two cherubim that are over the ark of the covenant law, I will meet with you and give you all my commands for the Israelites (Exodus 25:21–22).

The presence of God must go with us into our battles. Do not enter the battlefield of sickness without it. Do not enter the battlefield of relationship struggles without it. It would have been incredibly foolish for the Israelites to approach an enemy without God's presence, and it would be equally foolish for us to try to as well.

THE GREATEST WEAPON WE POSSESS

What happened next was the greatest revelation we can capture from the story of Jericho.

On the seventh day, they got up at daybreak and marched around the city seven times in the same manner, except that on that day they circled the city seven times. The seventh time around, when the priests sounded the trumpet blast, Joshua commanded the army, "Shout! For the Lord has given you the city!" (Joshua 6:15–16).

On that day in Canaan, it wasn't swords that brought down those walls. It wasn't vast armies or threats or politics. It was an instrument that can create life or death. The sharpest weapon in the Israelites' possession was not the sword but the tongue. The battle was won with their mouths as they lifted a shout. By the way, this wasn't just any shout. It wasn't a shout like you would hear at a sporting event or political rally. It was a shout of passion that cannot explained on any piece of paper. It was the kind of shout that could have only come from a group of people who had fought a much bigger fight before they ever walked up to the walls of Jericho. This shout had a foundation of 400 years of suffering in slavery and 40 years of wandering in the wilderness. It spoke of the deeply vulnerable process of allowing God to circumcise both their bodies and their hearts. It was a holy, passionate, thankful, and overjoyed shout in the natural that locked with the supernatural working of God to bring down physical walls.

There will be days you don't feel like worshipping. There will be days you don't feel like waiting. I've had plenty of those days myself. During those days, it can be difficult to remember what it's all for. Here is a formula you should write down, put on your bathroom mirror, and look at every morning to remind yourself. Ready? **Your waiting + your worship = your warship.** You're waiting for God to tear down your Jericho's walls. You've been obedient and marched around the enemy over and over and over again. Make this decision today: *While I wait, I will worship. It doesn't matter how long the waiting lasts. I won't stop worshipping.* People often think of worship as something that happens in church on Sunday mornings, but worship can happen anywhere. I can worship as I sit at my desk or walk around my neighborhood. I can worship while I'm changing a diaper or changing a tire.

In Acts 16, we read about Paul and Silas being put in prison after casting a demon out of a fortune teller. Verse 25 says, "About midnight Paul and Silas were praying and singing hymns to God." They worshipped while they waited. Another example is Daniel. When the Babylonians took the Israelites into exile, Daniel was one of the young Jewish men chosen to serve the king. He received a new name and special training, and he found favor with the king. However, despite all the attempts to assimilate him into Babylonian culture, Daniel did not forget who he really was. He believed God would one day deliver the Israelites back to their homeland, and while he was waiting, he chose to worship. "Three times a day he got down on his knees and prayed, giving thanks to his God" (Daniel 6:10).

Jesus waited in the Garden of Gethsemane to hear from His Father. He prayed, "My Father, if it is possible, may this cup be taken from me. Yet not as I will, but as you will" (Matthew 26:39). You know what that is? An act of worship. Worship doesn't require the use of your mouth or your hands. Worship is saying in your heart, "God, I surrender to You."

One of my favorite stories in the Bible is found in 2 Chronicles 20. This chapter begins with the Moabites and Ammonites coming to fight against King Jehoshaphat.

> Alarmed, Jehoshaphat resolved to inquire of the Lord, and he proclaimed a fast for all Judah. The people of Judah came together to seek help from the Lord; indeed, they came from every town in Judah to seek him (vv. 3–4).

The king and the people wait and worship, and God answers their desperate plea with this message:

You will not have to fight this battle. Take up your positions; stand firm and see the deliverance the Lord will give you, Judah and Jerusalem. Do not be afraid; do not be discouraged. Go out to face them tomorrow, and the Lord will be with you (v. 17).

Once again, God wants His people to know that He is with them. Yes, they still have to show up to the battlefield; no one gets to hide back in town. But even before they face the enemy, they begin wielding the same weapon used at the battle of Jericho. It's the same weapon you have for your battle too.

Jehoshaphat appointed men to sing to the Lord and to praise him for the splendor of his holiness as they went out at the head of the army, saying:
"Give thanks to the Lord,
    for his love endures forever" (2 Chronicles 20:21).

Leading the troops aren't men with swords, but men with praise. Jehoshaphat could have instructed them to beg God for mercy or favor; instead, he just wants them to worship. And watch what happens:

As they began to sing and praise, the Lord set ambushes against the men of Ammon and Moab and Mount Seir who were invading Judah, and they were defeated.
When the men of Judah came to the place that overlooks the desert and looked toward the vast army, they saw only dead bodies lying on the ground; no one had escaped (2 Chronicles 20:22, 24).

If you look closely at story after story in Scripture, you will begin to see the reoccurring theme of God's faithfulness and power. Yes, the details vary as to who is facing the battle, what circumstances have led them to that point, and who the enemy is. You may look at your own situation and think, *This is different than anything I have ever faced before. I don't see how God is going to come through for me this time.* Let me encourage you. God's faithfulness and power are not variables based on the details of a battle. His faithfulness and power are constants based on who He is—our unchanging, perfect heavenly Father who hears our prayers and responds, "I am with you."

TIMING IS EVERYTHING

If you have been a follower of Christ for very long, you have probably come to realize that God's timing is rarely the same as yours. Have you ever felt that if life didn't involve this little thing called *faith*, everything would be so much easier? (I'll admit I've had that thought.) But that would exclude the necessity for God in our lives. He never seems to be early, but He is also never late. He is rarely fast, but I have found that He is always steadfast. In all of the stories throughout Scripture, He shows up right on time. Just as Abraham is raising the knife to sacrifice his son, Isaac, God stops him and provides a ram for the burnt offering. Just as Pharaoh's army is approaching the Israelites, God splits the Red Sea, and His people walk across on dry ground.

Maybe you feel like the Israelites on their last march around Jericho. *Exhausted. Worn out.* You're on your last leg, your last hope, and your last pass. And you want to give up. Or perhaps you've already given up. Here's what I would say to you: it's the last pass that brings the walls down. Don't quit circling your problem. Keep waiting. Keep worshipping. Your worship will become the very thing God uses to defeat the enemy.

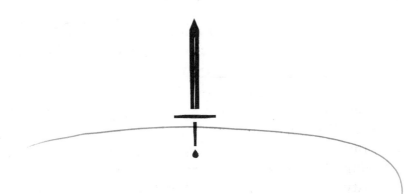

**Your worship will become the very thing
God uses to defeat the enemy.**

THE MIDDLE WATCH

For Gideon's army, the darkest night was the time for their greatest response. Judges 7:19 says, "Gideon and the hundred men with him reached the edge of the camp **at the beginning of the middle watch**, just after they had changed the guard" (bold added).

In those days there were three overnight watches. The middle watch started at 10 p.m. and lasted until 2 a.m. It was the middle of the night. So what did Gideon's army do in the dark? They shouted, they lifted their voices, and they praised God.

Maybe you have a hard time wrapping your brain around the idea of worshipping God in the middle of your darkest hour. It feels hard enough to get out of bed, much less do anything else. But here is the reason why the darkest hour is so important: it's the time when the enemy least expects you to do anything. In the darkest hour, Satan thinks he has you defeated. He believes he has you outnumbered. So he sits back, probably laughing and thinking, *This battle hasn't even started, and I've already won.*

You may be in the middle of your darkest hour right now. If so, it is time to pull out your most powerful weapon—your tongue. Start worshipping. If you aren't sure what to say, here are some Scriptures to help you get started.

> Yours, Lord, is the greatness and the power
> > and the glory and the majesty and the splendour,
> > for everything in heaven and earth is yours.
> Yours, Lord, is the kingdom;
> > You are exalted as head over all (1 Chronicles 29:11).

> Lord, you are my God;
> > I will exalt you and praise your name,

for in perfect faithfulness,
> you have done wonderful things,
> things planned long ago (Isaiah 25:1).

I will sing of the Lord's great love forever;
> with my mouth I will make your faithfulness known
> through all generations.
I will declare that your love stands firm forever,
> that you have established your faithfulness in heaven
> itself (Psalm 89:1–3).

CLOSING THOUGHTS

I remember when God brought fresh revelation to me about the topic of battles. I was up early writing a sermon, and suddenly, it was as if God took the pain of everyone who would ever hear this message or read this book and began to let me feel it. All the abandonment. All the abuse. All the rejection. All the shame. He let me experience the stench behind the stone. There at my desk at 4:30 in the morning, I began to weep uncontrollably. I didn't want to wake up my family (they probably would have thought I had lost my mind), but I was completely and utterly undone.

I know this book has been intense. It may not become an instant bestseller, because it doesn't have a "7 steps to a better you" or a "how to be blessed" theme. But I know that I know that I know that this was the burden that the Holy Spirit put on me. I preached this message at my church, and people flooded the altars. I went on to share it at other churches, chapel services, devotionals, and even one on ones with people. Every single time, God showed up and did a powerful work in people's lives.

Whatever your issue is, I'm asking you to respond. It does not mean that you have done something wrong but rather that you have been wronged. When you acknowledge the stench behind the stone, you're acknowledging that someone or something at some time in your life has inflicted pain on you. And I believe that God would say to you, "Today is the day I remove the reproach of that situation from you." Escort Jesus to your place of pain in the same way that Mary and Martha showed Jesus where they had buried theirs. Lay the stone of rejection down at the foot of the cross and turn it into a foundational cornerstone upon which God can build something beautiful in your life.

You don't have to do this alone. I highly encourage you to confide in a pastor, a licensed counselor, or a mature and godly friend who can walk with you on this journey of healing and wholeness. I believe Jesus will begin resurrecting the parts of your heart you thought were dead, just as He resurrected Lazarus. John 11:44 reads, "The dead man came out, his hands and feet bound in graveclothes, his face wrapped in a headcloth. Jesus told them, 'Unwrap him and let him go!'" (NLT). May you be loosed from the grip of the enemy and walk healthy and whole—the way you were intended to live.

I pray you feel the power and the presence of the Holy Spirit as I leave you with these words of blessing:

> The Lord bless you
>   and keep you;
> the Lord make his face shine on you
>   and be gracious to you;
> the Lord turn his face toward you
>   and give you peace (Numbers 6:24–26).

When you acknowledge the stench behind the stone, you're acknowledging that someone or something at some time in your life has inflicted pain on you.

Appendix 1

LEADER'S GUIDE

LEADER'S GUIDE

THE *HALF THE BATTLE* Leader's Guide is designed to help you lead your small group or class through the *Half the Battle* book. Use this guide along with the book for a life-changing, interactive experience. Of course, the Study Guide can also be used for individual review and study or one-on-one teaching.

BEFORE YOU MEET

- Ask God to prepare the hearts and minds of the people in your group. Ask Him to show you how to encourage each person to integrate the principles they discover through reading this book and group discussion into their daily lives.
- Before the meeting, read the chapter you will be discussing and familiarize yourself with that chapter's discussion and activation questions.

KEY TIPS FOR THE LEADER

- Generate participation and discussion.
- Resist the urge to teach. The goal is for great conversation that leads to discovery.
- Ask open-ended questions—questions that can't be answered with "yes" or "no" (e.g., "What do you think about that?" rather than "Do you agree?").

- When a question arises, ask the group for their input first, instead of immediately answering it yourself.
- Be comfortable with silence. If you ask a question and no one responds, rephrase the question and wait for a response. Your primary role is to create an environment where people feel comfortable to be themselves and participate, not to provide the answers to all of their questions.
- Ask the group to pray for each other from week to week, especially about key issues that arise during your group time. This is how you begin to build authentic community and encourage spiritual growth within the group.

KEYS TO A DYNAMIC SMALL GROUP

RELATIONSHIPS

Meaningful, encouraging relationships are the foundation of a dynamic small group. Teaching, discussion, worship, and prayer are important elements of a group meeting, but the depth of each element is often dependent upon the depth of the relationships among members.

AVAILABILITY

Building a sense of community within your group requires members to prioritize their relationships with one another. This means being available to listen, care for one another, and meet each other's needs.

MUTUAL RESPECT

Mutual respect is shown when members value each other's opinions (even when they disagree) and are careful never to put down or embarrass others in the group (including their spouses, who may or may not be present).

OPENNESS

A healthy small group environment encourages sincerity and transparency. Members treat each other with grace in areas of weakness, allowing each other room to grow.

CONFIDENTIALITY

To develop authenticity and a sense of safety within the group, each member must be able to trust that things discussed within the group will not be shared outside the group.

SHARED RESPONSIBILITY

Group members will share the responsibility of group meetings by using their God-given abilities to serve at each gathering. Some may greet, some may host, some may teach, etc. Ideally, each person should be available to care for others as needed.

SENSITIVITY

Dynamic small groups are born when the leader consistently seeks and is responsive to the guidance of the Holy Spirit, following His leading throughout the meeting as opposed to sticking to the "agenda." This guidance is especially important during the discussion and ministry time.

FUN!

Dynamic small groups take the time to have fun. Create an atmosphere for fun and be willing to laugh at yourself every now and then!

Appendix 2

STUDY GUIDE

Study Guide 1

BEFORE THE BATTLE

REVIEW

Most of us are engaged in a battle of some kind, or we soon will be in the future. It is not a word that most of us are fond of or comfortable with. Battles may be brief or drawn out, simple or complicated, but they are an inevitable part of life. Without a battle, there can be no victory.

The Israelites are a prime example of a people facing constant battles, both outwardly against foes like the Egyptians and the Amalekites as well as inwardly. They were a stubborn people as a whole, who had to be constantly rescued by a loving God—not unlike us today.

Before the Israelites could fight any physical enemies in the Promised Land, they had to fight the battle within and obey the Lord's command to circumcise themselves. Circumcision was instituted by God as a physical sign of His covenant relationship with His people, but it also represents the way God wants to deal with our hearts. We must be willing to allow Him to remove anything from our lives that will keep us from winning our battles.

KEY THOUGHT/CONCEPT

God wants to circumcise our hearts. We must open ourselves up and reveal our true selves—our emotions, our pains, and our fears. When we do so, He will remove the reproach of our past and enable us to move forward in victory over the enemy.

KEY SCRIPTURES

Genesis 17:10–11

This is my covenant with you and your descendants after you, the covenant you are to keep: Every male among you shall be circumcised. You are to undergo circumcision, and it will be the sign of the covenant between me and you.

Jeremiah 4:3–4

For thus says the Lord to the men of Judah and Jerusalem:
"Break up your fallow ground,
And do not sow among thorns.
Circumcise yourselves to the Lord,
And take away the foreskins of your hearts,
You men of Judah and inhabitants of Jerusalem,
Lest My fury come forth like fire
And burn so that no one can quench *it*
Because of the evil of your doings" (NKJV).

Romans 2:28–29

A person is not a Jew who is one only outwardly, nor is circumcision merely outward and physical. No, a person is a Jew who is one inwardly; and circumcision is circumcision of the heart, by the Spirit, not by the written code.

Luke 2:34–35

This child is destined to cause many in Israel to fall, and many others to rise. He has been sent as a sign from God, but many will oppose him. As a result, the deepest thoughts of many hearts will be revealed. And a sword will pierce your very soul.

Joshua 5:9

Then the Lord said to Joshua, "Today I have rolled away the shame of your slavery in Egypt." So that place has been called Gilgal to this day.

KEY QUOTES

The children of Israel fought an even greater battle *before* the walls of Jericho fell.

Before we ever win the battles in our future and take territory for our marriages, children, churches, finances, and careers, we must first win the greatest battle we will ever fight—the battle within!

If we begin to see people's issues as pain and not as personal attacks on us, then we can begin to offer real ministry.

DISCUSSION

QUESTION 1

What comes to your mind when you hear the word "battle"? How do you respond to the idea of having to face battles in your life?

_____

_____

_____

QUESTION 2

How do you think the Israelites felt when they were preparing to enter the Promised Land? What did they expect to happen after they entered?

_____

_____

_____

QUESTION 3

What was the real purpose and significance of circumcision, both to the Israelites and to us today as Christians? In your own words, what is "circumcision of the heart"?

_____

_____

_____

QUESTION 4

What are some things that God has cut away from your heart to bring you to Him? What are some things that He may still need to deal with?

_____

_____

_____

QUESTION 5

Why is it important to wait on God? What does it mean to learn to "wait well"? Do you think you are good at waiting? Explain or give some examples.

_____

_____

_____

QUESTION 6

What does "reproach" mean? Can you identify, either in yourself of someone you know well, how the pain of the past has caused an inappropriate reaction? Explain or give an example.

_____

_____

_____

ACTIVATION

- Consider how you feel about the battles you are likely to face and ask God to help you prepare your heart for them.
- Identify some pain from your past and ask God to help you deal with it and remove the reproach.

PRAYER

Heavenly Father, we praise You for always being with us in our battles. We thank You for the covenant promise of circumcision, and we proclaim that we are Your people. We commit to allowing You to cut away the foreskin of our hearts so that You can take away the reproach of our past and help us win the battle within. We commit to being a people of patient faith. Help us face our battles with confidence so that we can bring Jesus to the world. In Jesus' name, Amen.

Study Guide 2

THE STENCH BEHIND THE STONE

REVIEW

After the Israelites cross the Jordan River into the Promised Land and circumcise themselves, the Lord says He has "rolled away the reproach of Egypt from [them]" (Joshua 5:9). The Lord names the place *Gilgal*, which means 'circle of stones' or 'rolled away.'

One biblical story where a stone was rolled away from the tomb is the story of Lazarus in John 11. Jesus delays and arrives four days after Lazarus dies. When considering opening the tomb, Martha comments about the "stench." The stench was not just the smell; it was also the pain in their souls. The stench represents issues that we hide internally and try to avoid.

Jesus is not okay with permanently sealed tombs. He comes to confront the stone we have rolled in front of our hearts and overcome the darkness. We must take Jesus to the place of our pain so that He can help us deal with it. No matter what the issue is or how long we have hidden it away, He can heal us if we will let Him.

KEY THOUGHT/CONCEPT

Like Mary and Martha, we often put our pain away in a dark place. We must allow Jesus to help us deal with our pain.

KEY SCRIPTURES

John 11:33–41

Therefore, when Jesus saw her weeping, and the Jews who came with her weeping, He groaned in the spirit and was troubled. And He said, "Where have you laid him?"

They said to Him, "Lord, come and see."

Jesus wept. Then the Jews said, "See how He loved him!"

And some of them said, "Could not this Man, who opened the eyes of the blind, also have kept this man from dying?"

Then Jesus, again groaning in Himself, came to the tomb. It was a cave, and a stone lay against it. Jesus said, "Take away the stone."

Martha, the sister of him who was dead, said to Him, "Lord, by this time there is a stench, for he has been *dead four days.*"

Jesus said to her, "Did I not say to you that if you would believe you would see the glory of God?" Then they took away the stone *from the place* where the dead man was lying. And Jesus lifted up *His* eyes and said, "Father, I thank You that You have heard Me (NKJV).

1 Kings 19:3–4, 11–12

Elijah was afraid and ran for his life. When he came to Beersheba in Judah, he left his servant there, while he himself went a day's journey into the wilderness. He came to a broom bush, sat down under it and prayed that he might die. "I have had enough, Lord," he said. "Take my life; I am no better than my ancestors." . . .

The Lord said, "Go out and stand on the mountain in the presence of the Lord, for the Lord is about to pass by." Then a great and powerful wind tore the mountains apart and shattered the rocks before the Lord, but the Lord was not in the wind. After the wind there was an earthquake, but the Lord was not in the earthquake. After the earthquake came a fire, but the Lord was not in the fire. And after the fire came a gentle whisper.

Jeremiah 17:9–10

The heart is hopelessly dark and deceitful,
>a puzzle that no one can figure out.
But I, God, search the heart
>and examine the mind.
I get to the heart of the human.
>I get to the root of things.
I treat them as they really are,
>not as they pretend to be (MSG).

KEY QUOTES

What do we do with things that carry a stench in our lives?. . . We shove them in a dark place in our heart and roll a stone in front of it.

Circumcision of the heart is a **continual** process, not a one-and-done event.

There is one thing that is for certain: if we ever want to be healed, we have to deal with the pain.

DISCUSSION

QUESTION 1

In John 11:21, Mary and Martha tell Jesus that if He had been there, Lazarus would not have died. When had Mary and Martha sent for Jesus? Why do you think they reacted the way they did in this verse?

_____

_____

_____

QUESTION 2

What is the worst smell (stench) that you have ever experienced? How did you react to it?

_____

_____

_____

QUESTION 3

How do you respond to past hurts or trauma? Is there a specific situation that continues to trouble you? Explain.

_____

_____

_____

QUESTION 4

Why is Satan so happy when we let a stone remain in place over the pain in our hearts?

_____

_____

_____

QUESTION 5

What did Jesus do _instead_ of criticizing, rebuking, or teaching Mary and Martha after they took Him to the place where their faith had ended?

_____

_____

_____

QUESTION 6

Why does Jesus not just remove or destroy the stone in front of the tomb of Lazarus Himself? Describe the part we need to play in dealing with our pain and compare that to God's part in the process.

_____

_____

_____

ACTIVATION

- Ask God to reveal an area of pain within yourself that you need to deal with.
- Pray that God will reveal the steps you need to take in order to deal with the pain.

PRAYER

Father in heaven, we praise You and thank You that You are willing to come alongside us and help us deal with the pain in our lives. We give You permission to go to the deepest parts of our hearts. Help us reveal to You our deepest needs. Continue to circumcise our hearts as we set aside our pride so that we can be healed. Thank You for Your grace and mercy. In Jesus' name, Amen.

Study Guide 3

DEALING WITH REJECTION

REVIEW

The devil is a deceiver, and one of his primary weapons against believers is rejection. Rejection often starts from a small seed of infection, just like many of the world's most serious diseases. That seed may be a harsh spoken word or a brief abusive action by a loved one. We humans are the primary carriers of the seed of rejection.

Rejection was one of the fundamental reasons why circumcision in the Old Testament was so important. Circumcision reminded the people of Israel of God's covenant relationship with them, and that He would never leave or forsake them. It was a symbol of hope and acceptance.

Rejection is a disease of the heart that develops roots of bitterness and unforgiveness. The fruit of rejection is often anger and aggression, which grows in the soil of fear and manifests itself in insecurity. Insecurity then produces a variety of bad fruit. Jesus is the only key we can use to open our hearts so that we can receive God's love, healing, and acceptance.

KEY THOUGHT/CONCEPT

Rejection is a seed of the devil that results in a disease of the heart. God's love and acceptance can overcome rejection if we focus on giving Jesus access to our whole heart.

KEY SCRIPTURES

Genesis 17:10-11

This is my covenant with you and your descendants after you, the covenant you are to keep: Every male among you shall be circumcised. You are to undergo circumcision, and it will be the sign of the covenant between me and you.

Exodus 1:6-11

Now Joseph and all his brothers and all that generation died, but the Israelites were exceedingly fruitful; they multiplied greatly, increased in numbers and became so numerous that the land was filled with them.

Then a new king, to whom Joseph meant nothing, came to power in Egypt. "Look," he said to his people, "the Israelites have become far too numerous for us. Come, we must deal shrewdly with them or they will become even more numerous and, if war breaks out, will join our enemies, fight against us and leave the country."

So they put slave masters over them to oppress them with forced labor, and they built Pithom and Rameses as store cities for Pharaoh.

Genesis 27:37–41

Isaac said to Esau, "I have made Jacob your master and have declared that all his brothers will be his servants. I have guaranteed him an abundance of grain and wine—what is left for me to give you, my son?"

Esau pleaded, "But do you have only one blessing? Oh my father, bless me, too!" Then Esau broke down and wept.

Finally, his father, Isaac, said to him,

"You will live away from the richness of the earth,
    and away from the dew of the heaven above.
You will live by your sword,
    and you will serve your brother.
But when you decide to break free,
    you will shake his yoke from your neck."

From that time on, Esau hated Jacob because their father had given Jacob the blessing. And Esau began to scheme: "I will soon be mourning my father's death. Then I will kill my brother, Jacob" (NLT).

Matthew 22:36–38

"Teacher, which is the greatest commandment in the Law?" Jesus replied: "'Love the Lord your God with all your heart and with all your soul and with all your mind.' This is the first and greatest commandment."

KEY QUOTES

We humans are the primary carriers of the seed of rejection.

For the Israelites suffering in Egypt, the covenant of circumcision was more than a ritual or tradition. It was a symbol of hope and acceptance . . . We may never experience slavery like the Israelites did, but we still have lives that are full of rejection. That is why it is so important that we *continually* allow God to circumcise our hearts.

The question we must ask ourselves is this: *what part of our hearts are we still holding back from God?*

DISCUSSION

QUESTION 1

How is the seed of rejection in our lives similar to the origins and spread of the Bubonic Plague?

_____

_____

_____

QUESTION 2

Why did the Israelites need a continual reminder of God's love and their relationship with Him? What are some examples of when the people of Israel (as a nation or as individuals like David) failed and needed to be restored and reminded of their relationship with God?

_____

_____

_____

QUESTION 3

Rejection is a common emotional wound we all experience. What are some examples of rejection that have affected you or a loved one? What were the consequences of those situations?

_____

_____

_____

QUESTION 4

How does today's environment of immediate communication through Facebook, Twitter, and so forth, fuel the promotion of rejection? Give some examples.

_____

_____

_____

QUESTION 5

What are the two general types of people through which insecurity manifests itself? Consider yourself, someone you know, or someone well-known in the public sphere. Give some examples of their responses to criticism and/or rejection. What is your response to such behavior?

_____

_____

_____

ACTIVATION

- Consider how you respond to rejection and come up with a concrete step you can take to help you better identify and manage rejection.
- Consider some ways that you may be showing rejection to others. Be specific and pray about how you can be more accepting and show God's love to others.

PRAYER

Heavenly Father, we are grateful that You never reject Your people. We acknowledge the spirit of rejection. Help us resist the seed of the rejection that the enemy promotes and attacks us with. Help us be sensitive to others and promote acceptance by loving people the way Jesus loved. Reveal to us ways that we can give more of our hearts to You. In Jesus' name, Amen.

Study Guide 4

THE FINAL RESTING PLACE OF PAIN

REVIEW

It is one thing to search the heart and identify the pain that is represented by the stench behind the stone. But once we identify the devil's methods and the pain they produce, what do we do with that knowledge? Where do we go from there?

First, we must take our pain out of our subconscious and bring it into the light. Write it down on a sheet of paper or type it out on your electronic device.

It is important to understand that we are not alone. Almost every prominent biblical figure in both the Old and New Testaments experienced rejection that brought pain. Rejection does not mean that you have done something wrong. It means someone has wronged you. The pain is not your fault.

There are several ways people handle the pain of the heavy stone of rejection. When we decide to reject the devil's scheme of rejection, we can be free. We can lay down our burdens—and our pain—at the feet of Jesus.

KEY THOUGHT/CONCEPT

We all experience rejection. Jesus is the best example of being rejected, and He is also the best example to use to learn how to deal with rejection. We must learn to reject the rejection. The best option is to lay our pain down at the feet of Jesus.

KEY SCRIPTURES

1 Kings 18:22; 19:10; 19:18

Then Elijah said to them, "I am the only one of the Lord's prophets left." . . .

He replied, "I have been very zealous for the Lord God Almighty. The Israelites have rejected your covenant, torn down your altars, and put your prophets to death with the sword. I am the only one left, and now they are trying to kill me too." . . .

"Yet I reserve seven thousand in Israel—all whose knees have not bowed down to Baal and whose mouths have not kissed him."

Psalm 118:22–24

The stone the builders rejected
    has become the cornerstone;
the Lord has done this,
    and it is marvelous in our eyes.
The Lord has done it this very day;
    let us rejoice today and be glad.

Matthew 27:46

About three in the afternoon Jesus cried out in a loud voice, *"Eli, Eli, lema sabachthani?"* (which means "My God, my God, why have you forsaken me?").

Genesis 45:5; 50:20

And now, do not be distressed and do not be angry with yourselves for selling me here, because it was to save lives that God sent me ahead of you. . . .

You intended to harm me, but God intended it for good to accomplish what is now being done, the saving of many lives (NLT).

KEY QUOTES

It is important to take your pain out of your subconscious and bring it into the light.

Rejection is not a new thing. You are not alone in this.

When someone rejects you, you have to have the ability to reject their rejection.

The beauty of Christ, His Church, and everything we stand for was established on a stone called rejection.

DISCUSSION

QUESTION 1

Have you ever felt overwhelmed or unable to figure out how to handle the pain from your past? Explain.

_____

_____

_____

QUESTION 2

Write down some examples of rejection and pain you have experienced. Compare your feelings and response at the time of the circumstance to your feelings and perspective on it now. How are they similar or different?

_____

_____

_____

QUESTION 3

Choose two or three examples of biblical figures (other than Jesus) and write down how they responded to rejection. Which responses were appropriate and which ones were not? What were the results of those responses?

_____

_____

_____

QUESTION 4

Look at the long list of examples of rejection Jesus suffered. Which of these do you think pained Jesus the most? Why?

_____

_____

_____

QUESTION 5

What are the inappropriate options that we can employ to deal with our pain and rejection? Give an example or two of how you have tried to deal with rejection using one of these options.

_____

_____

_____

ACTIVATION

- Read through the story of Joseph and look at the methods he used to overcome rejection. How might you take and apply one or more of these approaches to deal with pain in your life?
- Ask the Holy Spirit how you might share this knowledge to help a loved one deal with the pain of rejection.

PRAYER

Father, we thank You for giving us a way to deal with our pain. The examples in Your Word show us how to put it away forever. Help us be like Joseph and be steadfast in serving You by serving others. Help us be like Paul and Barnabas in spreading the Word. We know that we are accepted by You even when we are rejected by others. We lay down our pain at Jesus' feet. In Jesus' name, Amen.

Study Guide 5

TIME TO TAKE GROUND

REVIEW

Once the Israelites crossed the Jordan River and entered the Promised Land, they had reached a milestone. However, reaching the Promised Land was just the beginning of their story. After a brief time of celebration (eating of the fruit of the land), they went right into the thick of a new battle, one which would be among the most famous in history.

World War I was a war fought from the trenches, and there are many similarities to the way we fight the enemy today. Satan comes after us with new weapons, so we hide in spiritual and emotional trenches, unaware that there are silent killers that can cause severe damage to our souls.

In Judges 6, the Israelites are on the verge of being wiped out by the Midianites, but God gives Gideon the courage to get out of his trench and engage the enemy. The Lord gives four impartations to this new leader: a new name, boldness, peace, and insulation. Like Gideon, we too can rise above our rejection, fear, and isolation to gain victory on the battlefield of our lives.

KEY THOUGHT/CONCEPT

The battle is most difficult when we live life in the trenches, like so many soldiers did in WWI. We cannot triumph in the trenches. Instead, we should learn from the example of Gideon how to rise above our rejection, fear, and isolation to become victorious believers.

KEY SCRIPTURES

Joshua 5:10–12

On the evening of the fourteenth day of the month, while camped at Gilgal on the plains of Jericho, the Israelites celebrated the Passover. The day after the Passover, that very day, they ate some of the produce of the land: unleavened bread and roasted grain. The manna stopped the day after they ate this food from the land; there was no longer any manna for the Israelites, but that year they ate the produce of Canaan.

Ephesians 6:12

For our struggle is not against flesh and blood, but against the rulers, against the authorities, against the powers of this dark world and against the spiritual forces of evil in the heavenly realms.

Judges 6:12–16, 22

The angel of the Lord appeared to him and said, "Mighty hero, the Lord is with you!"

"Sir," Gideon replied, "if the Lord is with us, why has all this happened to us? And where are all the miracles our ancestors told us about? Didn't they say, 'The Lord brought us up out of Egypt'? But now the Lord has abandoned us and handed us over to the Midianites."

Then the Lord turned to him and said, "Go with the strength you have, and rescue Israel from the Midianites. I am sending you!"

"But Lord," Gideon replied, "how can I rescue Israel? My clan is the weakest in the whole tribe of Manasseh, and I am the least in my entire family!"

The Lord said to him, "I will be with you. And you will destroy the Midianites as if you were fighting against one man." . . . When Gideon realized that it was the angel of the Lord, he cried out, "Oh, Sovereign Lord, I'm doomed! I have seen the angel of the Lord face to face!" (NLT).

Joshua 1:5

No one will be able to stand against you all the days of your life. As I was with Moses, so I will be with you; I will never leave you nor forsake you.

KEY QUOTES

We were never meant to sit back and enjoy the fruit of Jesus without using it to take ground from the enemy.

Perhaps no one is firing bullets at us, but our jobs, families, responsibilities, and strains have a way of firing some pretty nasty stress and worry our way.

If we look closely enough at our own lives, we can find that our own trenches are laced with silent killers.

God isn't okay with Gideon staying in his trench, and He isn't okay with you staying in yours either.

DISCUSSION

QUESTION 1

The Israelites celebrated the Passover when they crossed over and camped at Gilgal. Put yourself in that place and time. What do you think the majority of the people were thinking and feeling at that time? How do you think you would feel? Why?

_____

_____

_____

QUESTION 2

What were some of the changes or differences in warfare that came about in WWI? Why did those changes drive troops into the trenches?

_____

_____

_____

QUESTION 3

What were some of the "silent killers" in the trenches of WWI? What parts of the body are they associated with? Which of these do you identify with the most in your life and why?

_____

_____

_____

QUESTION 4

Why can troops (believers) not triumph in the trenches? Explain in your own words, in the context of a spiritual war.

_____

_____

_____

QUESTION 5

What are the four impartations that God gives to Gideon? Which of these do you need most in your own fight on the spiritual battlefield? Why?

_____

_____

_____

ACTIVATION

- Ask the Holy Spirit to show you what area of difficulty in the trenches you need to most deal with, and then ask for the power to deal with it.
- With the help of the Holy Spirit, develop a "battle plan" to take ground, using the example of Gideon and the impartations God gave him.

PRAYER

Father in heaven, we praise You for providing us with everything we need, like You did for the Israelites. Help us recognize when we are suffering from the diseases of the trenches in our spiritual battle. Give us the impartations You gave Gideon. We want to be mighty heroes in Your kingdom battles. Make us bold in your Spirit. Give us peace, freedom from fear, and the joy of Your abiding presence. In Jesus' name, Amen.

Study Guide 6

THE WEAPON FOR WAR

REVIEW

Whether or not you have fully prepared yourself for battle, you will eventually have to face a hardship in life—your spiritual version of the battle with the Midianites.

The story of Gideon shows the three distinct items we must carry into our battlefield to be victorious. First is the torch, which is Jesus. He is the light that guides our steps. Second is the trumpet. God calls us to unity, like He summoned the Israelites to corporate prayer, worship, and battle. We must stand together against our enemy. Third is the tongue. It may well be our greatest weapon. We see the power of the tongue—giving praise and worship to God—in Judges 7:20–21. Praise and worship usher in God's presence in our lives.

The battle of Jericho was won with a shout of praise that was a response to the Spirit's leading. Sometimes, like in Jericho, we have to wait before we get to see the victory. No matter how long it takes or what obstacles we encounter, we must never stop worshipping.

God's timing is rarely the same as ours, but it is always perfect. Gideon's response and call to battle came in the middle of the night. When we worship in the darkest hour, the enemy will least expect it. The Holy Spirit will lead you to victory.

KEY THOUGHT/CONCEPT

We will eventually have to face our enemies. The torch of Jesus, the unity expressed by the call of the trumpet, and the tongue of praise are our three main weapons. Perhaps the most powerful of these is the tongue of praise and worship, which ushers in the presence and power of God to our lives.

Together we can acknowledge our pain, lay down our rejection at the feet of Jesus, and, like Gideon, face our battles victoriously.

KEY SCRIPTURES

Judges 7:19–22

Gideon and the hundred men with him reached the edge of the camp at the beginning of the middle watch, just after they had changed the guard. They blew their trumpets and broke the jars that were in their hands. The three companies blew the trumpets and smashed the jars. Grasping the torches in their left hands and holding in their right hands the trumpets they were to blow, they shouted, "A sword for the Lord and for Gideon!" While each man held his position around the camp, all the Midianites ran, crying out as they fled.

When the three hundred trumpets sounded, the Lord caused the men throughout the camp to turn on each other with their swords. The army fled to Beth Shittah toward Zererah as far as the border of Abel Meholah near Tabbath.

John 12:46

I have come into the world as a light, so that no one who believes in me should stay in darkness.

Proverbs 18:21

The tongue has the power of life and death,
     and those who love it will eat its fruit.

Acts 16:25

About midnight Paul and Silas were praying and singing hymns to God, and the other prisoners were listening to them.

KEY QUOTES

Whether the issue will involve your career, family, health, finances, or something else, you can start getting ready today in order to win the battle tomorrow.

If you do not have the light of Christ with you, then you are just wandering around in the darkness.

Your waiting + your worship = your warship.

DISCUSSION

QUESTION 1

How does Jesus act as a lamp to our feet and a light to our path?

_____

_____

_____

QUESTION 2

Read John 17:20–22. The common denominator of the trumpet call at Gilgal was unity. How unified is the Church as a whole today? How unified is your local church? What could you do to help create unity among your community of believers or family?

_____

_____

_____

QUESTION 3

The tongue has the power to create and to destroy. In what ways have you used your tongue destructively? Why do you think you acted that way?

_____

_____

_____

QUESTION 4

Your waiting + your worship = your warship. What does this mean to you, in your own words?

_____

_____

_____

QUESTION 5

Read 1 Chronicles 29:11, Isaiah 25:1, and Psalm 89:1–3. How do these passages inspire you to start worshipping?

_____

_____

_____

ACTIVATION

- Ask the Holy Spirit to show you ways you can be a tool of unity in your church. Share those with your family or fellow believers.
- Identify some specific ways and times you can use your tongue in worship and take the first step to win the battle.

PRAYER

Heavenly Father, I am ready to head into battle with the enemy. Help me identify those areas of conflict and provide me with the weapons I need. May Your Holy Spirit lead me to keep the light of Jesus shining in my life. May I recognize every opportunity for a trumpet call to provide unity. May my tongue and voice be raised in worship to You every day. In Your timing and through Your Spirit, I know I can win the believer's battle. In Jesus name, Amen.

NOTES

1. C. S. Lewis, *The Problem of Pain* (New York: HarperOne, 2015), 91.
2. History.com Editors, "Black Death," History.com (A&E Television Networks, June 6, 2019), https://www.history.com/topics/middle-ages/black-death.
3. The Editors of Encyclopaedia Britannica, "Alexandre Yersin," Encyclopædia Britannica (Encyclopædia Britannica, inc., September 19, 2019), https://www.britannica.com/biography/Alexandre-Yersin).
4. History.com Editors, "Black Death".
5. Becky Little, "Rats Didn't Spread the Black Death-It Was Humans," History.com (A&E Television Networks, August 30, 2018), https://www.history.com/news/rats-didnt-spread-the-black-death-it-was-humans.
6. Melissa Conrad Stöppler, "Plague (Black Death) Definition, Symptoms, Types, Treatment, History," (MedicineNet, November 27, 2019), https://www.medicinenet.com/plague_facts/article.htm.
7. "Plague," Mayo Clinic (Mayo Foundation for Medical Education and Research, February 5, 2019), https://www.mayoclinic.org/diseases-conditions/plague/symptoms-causes/syc-20351291.
8. Guy Winch, "Why Rejection Hurts so Much - and What to Do about It," (ideas.ted.com, December 8, 2015), https://ideas.ted.com/why-rejection-hurts-so-much-and-what-to-do-about-it.
9. Kirsten Weir, "Science Watch: The Pain of Social Rejection," *Monitor on Psychology* 43, no. 4 (2012): p. 50, https://www.apa.org/monitor/2012/04/rejection.
10. Guy Winch, "10 Surprising Facts About Rejection," Psychology Today (Sussex Publishers, July 3, 2013), https://www.psychologytoday.com/us/blog/the-squeaky-wheel/201307/10-surprising-facts-about-rejection.
11. Kirsten Weir, "Science Watch: The Pain of Social Rejection".
12. Guy Winch, "10 Surprising Facts About Rejection".
13. Ibid.
14. Guy Winch, "Why Rejection Hurts so Much - and What to Do about It".

15. Battle of the Somme Ends, History.com, accessed February 10, 2020, https://www.history.com/this-day-in-history/battle-of-the-somme-ends.

16. Voices of the First World War: The Submarine War, Imperial War Museum podcast, June 5, 2018, https://www.iwm.org.uk/history/voices-of-the-first-world-war-the-submarine-war.

17. First Trenches are Dug on the Western Front, History.com, accessed February 10, 2020, https://www.history.com/this-day-in-history/first-trenches-are-dug-on-the-western-front.

18. Caroline Alexander, "World War I: 100 Years Later: The Shock of War," *Smithsonian Magazine*, September 2010), accessed February 10, 2020, https://www.smithsonianmag.com/history/the-shock-of-war-55376701/.

19. Ibid.

20. Ibid.

21. Malaria in Wars and Victims, accessed February 10, 2020, https://www.malariasite.com/wars-victims/.

22. Canadian War Museum online, accessed February 10, 2020, https://www.warmuseum.ca/firstworldwar/history/life-at-the-front/trench-conditions/rats-lice-and-exhaustion/.

ABOUT THE AUTHOR

DR. JON CHASTEEN is president of The King's University in Southlake, Texas. He holds a Bachelors of Science from Southwestern Christian University, a Masters in Education from the University of Central Oklahoma, and a Doctorate in Education from Oral Roberts University. Jon began his career in higher education at Southwestern Christian University, where he served as vice president for Advancement for six years.

In addition to his educational leadership experience, Jon has served in pastoral ministry since 2011. He and his wife, Michele, serve as the lead pastors of Victory Church in Oklahoma City, Oklahoma. Jon's greatest passion is to empower and equip the local church to live, move, and be in the fullness of Christ. He truly believes that the local church is the hope of the world and desires to lead with transparency, authenticity, and passion. Jon enjoys traveling and speaking at churches and conferences, and he also hosts the podcast Church InTension.

Jon and Michele have been married for almost 20 years, and they have two children, Corey and Jace.